CROSSING
THE RIVER

*One Man's Journey From
Darkness to Light*

T. CHER MOUA

Inspiring Voices books may be ordered through booksellers or by contacting:

Inspiring Voices
1663 Liberty Drive
Bloomington, IN 47403
www.inspiringvoices.com
1-(866) 697-5313

Unless otherwise identified, Scripture quotations are taken from The
Holy Bible, New International Version Copyright© 1973, 1978,
1984 by the International Bible Society and published by special
arrangement with Zondervan Publishing House, Grand Rapids, MI.

ISBN: 978-1-4624-0470-4 (sc)
ISBN: 978-1-4624-0469-8 (e)

Library of Congress Control Number: 2013901107

Printed in the United States of America

Inspiring Voices rev. date: 1/24/2013

TABLE OF CONTENTS

T. Cher & Mai Yia

T. Cher & Mai Yia with their adult children: from left in the back – Pa Houa, Cheng, Josh, Hnou, and Hli

Note to the reader: Right away the reader will notice that this genogram is incomplete. Notice that none of the maternal side is mentioned in this graph. The purpose is not to view all maternal sides as unimportant. Rather, it is intended to demonstrate the author's biological connection with Muas Num Vwg. The author faces one major challenge in putting this genogram together: there were no written records of any of the great-great grandparents, great grandparents or their in-laws. So in this attempt to trace the author's biological connection to his great-great grandfather he can only put down the paternal side of the family. It is the author's hope to continue research in the days ahead into his maternal heritage and find a complete connection with his great-great grandparents and extended family.

The reader will also notice that most of the names of the individuals appear in this genogram are in Hmong. It is the author's intention to retain the traditional Hmong name where possible to reflect accurate spelling and pronunciation of each of the names.

Please also note the variance of the author's name as follow: The author's anglicized name is "Cher" with the initial "T." The author's birth/given name is Cher which, if translated, means "Wine." And the initial "T" is "Txhaj" which translated to mean "Treasure." Txhaj Cawv means "Treasured Wine." With this short explanation, the author hopes to clarify some potential confusion surrounding the author's name and relationship in the genogram.

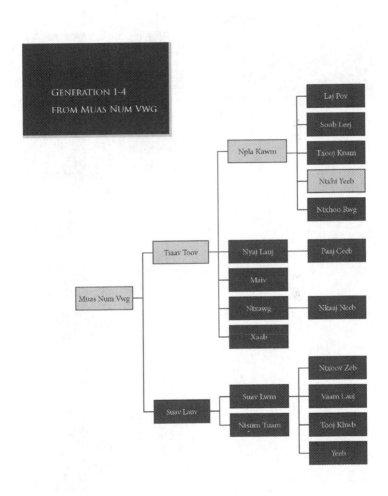

GENERATION 1-4
FROM MUAS NUM VWG

- Muas Num Vwg
  - Tsaav Toov
    - Npla Kawm
      - Laj Pov
      - Soob Leej
      - Txooj Kuam
      - Ntxhi Yeeb
      - Ntxhoo Rwg
    - Nyaj Lauj
      - Paaj Ceeb
    - Maiv
    - Ntxawg
      - Nkaaj Nceb
    - Xaab
  - Suav Lauv
    - Suav Lwm
      - Ntxoov Zeb
      - Vaam Lauj
      - Tooj Khwb
      - Yeeb
    - Ntsum Tuam

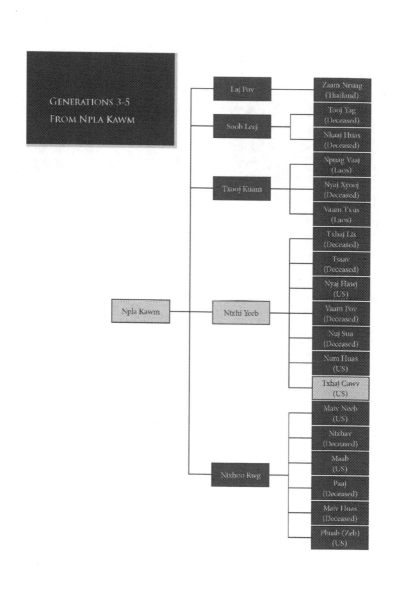

Generations 3–5
From Npla Kawm

Npla Kawm

Laj Pov — Zuam Nruag (Thailand)

Soob Leej — Tooj Yag (Deceased)
Nkaaj Huas (Deceased)

Txooj Kuam — Npuag Vaaj (Laos)
Nyaj Xyooj (Deceased)
Vaam Txus (Laos)

Ntxhi Yeeb — Txhaj Lis (Deceased)
Tsaav (Deceased)
Nyaj Hawj (US)
Vaam Pov (Deceased)
Nuj Sua (Deceased)
Num Huas (US)
Txhaj Cawv (US)

Ntxhoo Rwg — Maiv Neeb (US)
Ntxhav (Deceased)
Maab (US)
Paaj (Deceased)
Maiv Huas (Deceased)
Phuab (Zeb) (US)

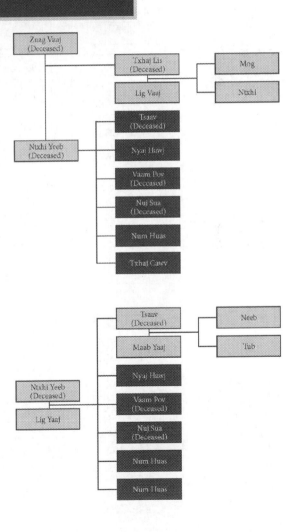

GENERATION 4-7
FROM NIXHI YEEB

Zuag Vaaj
(Deceased)

Txhaj Lis
(Deceased)

Mog

Lig Vaaj

Ntxhi

Nixhi Yeeb
(Deceased)

Tsaav
(Deceased)

Nyaj Hawj

Vaam Pov
(Deceased)

Nuj Sua
(Deceased)

Num Huas

Txhaj Cawv

Nixhi Yeeb
(Deceased)

Lig Yaaj

Tsaav
(Deceased)

Neeb

Maab Yaaj

Tub

Nyaj Hawj

Vaam Pov
(Deceased)

Nuj Sua
(Deceased)

Num Huas

Num Huas

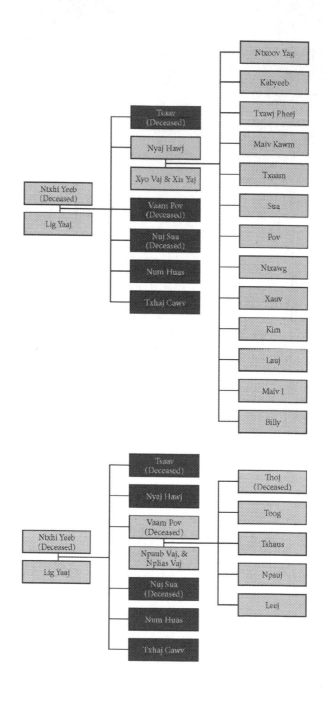

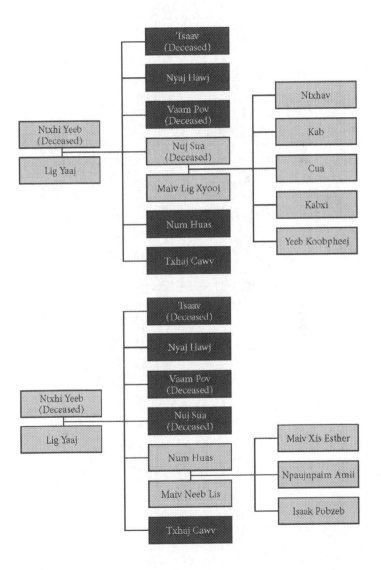

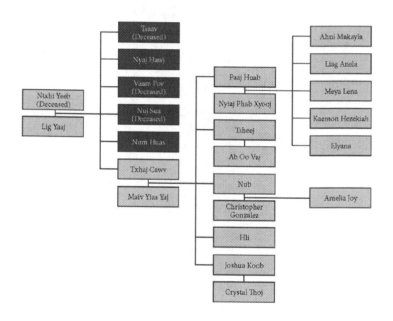

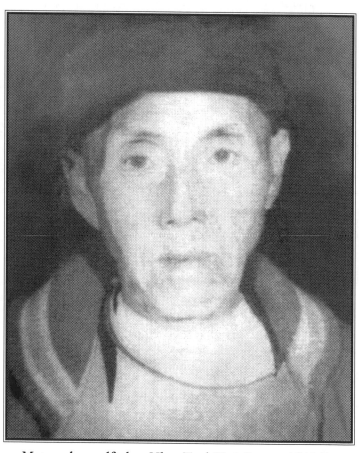

Maternal grandfather, Nkag Tswb Yaaj, Laos, mid 1960s

TIMELINE OF EVENTS

Event 1: 1967 – Starting elementary school in the village of Ban Phou Huard, Xiengkhouang, Laos

Event 2: April 1969 –Starting evacuation and became refugee as Communist troops invaded the region

Event 3: September 1969 – the death of Tsaav, big brother and father-figure, outside of the regional military headquarters Meuong Mok's Mount 50

Event 4: May 1975 – the fall of Laos and Vietnam

Event 5: May 1977 – first attempt to cross the Mekong River (but failed)

Event 6: September 22, 1978 – Crossing the River (successfully)

Event 7: June 24, 1979 – Journey to America began (Day long bus ride from Nongkhai to Bangkok)

Event 8:   June 27, 1979 – Boarding 747 Jetliner (for the first time) to America, the Land of the Unknown

Event 9:   June 29, 1979 – Stepping into American soil at Washington International Airport

Event 10:   July 1979 – Leaving for Pittsburgh, PA via Bus

Event 11:   September 1979 – Enrolled at Allegheny High School as a tenth grader

Event 12:   December 13, 1980 – Accepted Christ and was baptized at Allegheny Center Alliance Church, Pittsburgh, PA

Event 13:   January 3, 1982 – Married Mai Yia Yang

Event 14:   June 30, 1982 – Graduated from Allegheny High School

Event 15:   August 24, 1982 – the birth of our first child – Pa Houa

Event 16:   June 10, 1983 – Leaving for Bible College, Toccoa Falls, GA

Event 17:   December 19, 1983 – the birth of our second child – Cheng

Event 18:   January 15, 1985 – the birth of our third child – Hnou

Event 19:   April 21, 1987 – the birth of our fourth child- Hli

Event 20: May 7, 1987 – Graduated from Toccoa Falls College with BS in Bible/Theology

Event 21: June 10, 1987 – Called to the Pastorate and moved for Detroit, MI

Event 22: July 10, 1987 – First day of pastoral ministry in Detroit, MI

Event 23: January 9, 1990 – the birth of our fifth child – Joshua Kong

Event 24: June 29, 1990 – Last day of pastoral work in Detroit, MI

Event 25: July 5, 1990 – First day of Church Planting in St. Paul, MN

Event 26: September 1990 – Hmong Faith Baptist Church was founded in St. Paul, MN through the support of Calvary Baptist Church under the leadership of Drs. Rich Shoenert and Sid Veenstra.

Event 27: April 1992 – The Bush Foundation Leadership Fellows Program Mid-career studies was awarded for graduate studies at Bethel Seminary, St. Paul.

Event 28: May 30, 1994 – Graduated from Bethel Theological Seminary, St. Paul

Event 29: December 27, 1995 – the inception of Family & Youth Advancement Services, Inc.

Event 30: December 15, 1997 – Became fulltime staff at Family & Youth Advancement Services, Inc.

Event 31: January 6, 2000 – Brother Vaam Pov passed away from a fall from his Manufactured Home rooftop in Menomonie, WI

Event 32: September 11, 2001 – Terrorist Attacks America (New York and Washington, DC)

Event 33: January 2004 – Accepted the call to plant CrossCultural EFC in the Upper Eastside of St. Paul with Pastor Michael Rice

Event 34: May 11, 2004 – Brother Nuj Sua passed away with cancer in St. Paul, MN

Event 35: February 15, 2005 – FYASI merged with the Union Gospel Mission, becoming Asian Ministries of the Union Gospel Mission Twin Cities

Pa Houa and her husband Nyiaj Phab with their children: front left – Meya Lena, Kaemon Hezekiah, Elyana, Anela Liag Back – Ahni Makayla Not pictured – Kailee Hadassah

DEDICATION

This book is dedicated to several people important in my life. First, to my late father whose life ended so prematurely in the early sixties in the countryside of Laos without seeing the journey or experiencing the struggles, sorrows, successes and joys of his seven sons from a life of destitution in and during the conflicts in Laos to a life of transition in Thailand and eventually in the United States of America. With great gratitude, I thank God for him for being instrumental in bringing me and my brothers into the world and serving as a father for a time.

To my mother who faithfully dedicated her life to nurturing and comforting her children through the good times and the bad, peace and war, in times of joy and sorrow, including the death of her husband and three of her sons. She made a decision early on after my father's passing away not to engage in any romantic relationship but to remain committed to being Mom to us as we journeyed through the years.

To my older brothers – Tsaav, Nyaj Hawj, Vaam Pov, Nuj Sua, and Num Huas, for their commitment to each other and our family. There is a Hmong saying, "Namtxiv sis tshe sis ntaus taag tsis nrauj lub txaag, kwvtij sis tshe sis ntaus taag tsis nrauj tug dlaab" which, translated means "Couples may argue and fight, but do not divide the bed; brothers may argue and fight, but do not divide religion." Let me put it slightly differently: Couples may argue and fight, but in the end they want to make things right; brothers may argue and fight, but in the end our biological connection is what makes us bind.

And to my nephews and nieces. I am humbled to be associated with you and to stand as a father figure for you through times of challenges and joys. I count it an honor and blessing from the Lord God for me to have a small part in your lives, which I hope has made your journey so far a little richer and more meaningful.

To my Pastor and spiritual father, Dr. Maurice R. Irvin and his wife, Darolyn Irvin (who passed away a few years before the writing of this Memoir), and to Ken and Nancy Fraser, enduring friends and mentors in my and my family's spiritual journeys. Your unconditional love and care for me, a stranger from who knows where, and your sharing your lives and resources in an attempt to disciple me in the ways and things of the Lord God has made, and continues to make, a life-altering impact on me. I am forever grateful.

To Larry Carlson, friend of Hmong refugees and corporate leader with a compassionate and generous heart. With your

Christ-centered love for the Hmong and your generous financial support, Family & Youth Advancement Services, Inc., was born in 1995 and continues to serve Hmong families in St. Paul, sharing the love of Christ in tangible ways. Lives have been touched and transformed because of your compassionate generosity. Thank you.

To Jay Bennett, President of the Wallestad Foundation, and to the foundation's benefactors. Through your friendship and generous financial support, Family & Youth Advancement Services, Inc,. survived and succeeded in the midst of and after the 911 events that forced many small non-profit organizations, including ministries, to fold. Your vision and mission has led the Hmong family to a brighter future.

To my wife, life-long ministry partner and soul mate who supported me through my education and ministry journeys over the years. Without your enduring love and patience in raising our five children while I pursued my theological education at Toccoa Falls College and Bethel Theological Seminary, I would not have been able to accomplish what I have up to this point. Thank you. I am forever grateful for your loving partnership.

To my children and grandchildren. You are the challenge and joy of my life. I thank God for allowing me to be your father for a time and giving me the responsibility to nurture, train, guide, and counsel you as my children. I am grateful to the Lord God for allowing me to have a part in your physical and spiritual growth to a point. May this memoir serve as a reminder for all of you and your children, grandchildren, and future generations who your ancestors were and where they came from and how they got here. History is a mirror. It provides a rearview into the journey of your heritage. As you see the trail of the history of your roots, I pray you will make better decisions about your present life-situations and navigate your way into the future.

Without a knowledge and understanding of one's past, it is impossible to move forward in meaningful ways. I pray that the Lord, God of Abraham, God of Isaac, and God of Jacob, the God who so loved the world, including such a refugee as me, would guide and protect you in your going out and coming in, and that he would watch over you. In short:

"The Lord bless you and keep you;
The Lord make his face shine upon
you and be gracious to you;
The Lord turn his face toward you and give you peace."

Numbers 6:24-26

For "…he who began a good work in you will carry it on to completion until the day of Christ Jesus" – Phil. 1:6b.

To him who is able to keep you from falling and to present you before his glorious presence without fault and with great joy—25to the only God our Savior be glory, majesty, power and authority, through Jesus Christ our Lord, before all ages, now and forevermore! Amen – Jude vv. 24-25.

INTRODUCTION

Two things my parents taught my siblings and me while growing up in the 1960s and 1970s were "Never kneel down to dine because if you do, you will become a slave of the Chinese," and "Don't cry too loud because if you do, the Chinese will come and cut out your gallbladder." I never quite understood those two warnings, but my siblings and I took them to heart and behaved very well. We actually believed that if we knelt while reclining at the table, we would become a Chinese slave, and if we cried loud enough, our cries would be heard and the Chinese would come and literally, surgically remove one's gallbladder.

Until recently when I read about a possible Hmong homeland in central China and the conflicts which resulted when Hmong migrated into Southeast Asia and eventually scattered around the world after the conclusion of the Vietnam Conflict in the 1970s, did I understand the meaning of those warnings. According to some scholars and Asian historians, there was a Hmong kingdom situated in China's Hebei province circa 3000 BC. There were constant conflicts between the Han Chinese and the Hmong. Eventually the Hmong subjects betrayed their king to the Chinese, he was captured and burned at the stake, and the Hmong were targeted for extermination. As a result, Hmong were driven southward out of China.

Also, there is a ritual practiced in the Hmong burial ceremony which symbolizes a sense of fear of the Chinese ingrained into the Hmong consciousness. Hmong bury their dead in two distinctive fashions: One is called "Hmong" style and the other "Chinese" style. The Hmong grave style is a mound of dirt stretching horizontally across a hillside without any elaborate decorations, while the Chinese grave style is set vertically on a slope of a hill and decorated with rocks and stones with raised "front" and a door in the center, apparently copycatting the Chinese grave to avoid any Chinese digging.

This was done because there were constant conflicts between the Chinese and the Hmong. Because the Hmong "rebellions" were so difficult to suppress and control, once the Chinese gained the upper hand over the Hmong, they took great efforts to make sure that a Hmong uprising would never be an issue again. The way to control the Hmong insurgency, the Chinese believed, was by population control through a selective process – exterminating every male, and forcing cross-ethnic marriage for all Hmong women to Chinese men. In addition, Chinese troops would dig up every Hmong grave they encountered.

This grave-digging was done so much so by the Chinese to the point where Hmong could no longer bear the vicious behavior of the Chinese. Hmong leaders and elders came up with the idea to counter these vicious and inhumane behaviors by burying their dead in Chinese fashion. Thus, the Hmong graves that were constructed in Chinese fashion were spared from being dug up so viciously. As time passed, this practice became ingrained in Hmong consciousness and culture, and it is a part of Hmong religious practice to this day.

Another religious practice that has been ingrained in the consciousness of the Hmong and is still being practiced by many in the Muas Num Vwg family is refusing to sacrifice buffalo for the dead. For my great, great grandfather Muas Num Vwg's descendents, many of whom still hold on to traditional Hmong animist beliefs even to the present day, buffalo sacrifice is forbidden at funerals. The story goes that when Muas Num Vwg's family (or his ancestors) fled from the Chinese, they came upon a grazing buffalo herd as they were being pursued. The leader of the fleeing band begged the buffalos to come to their defense and protection. And the buffalos did.

After the band of the refugees was rescued, the leader went back to the buffalos and made a covenant with the animals, saying that since they had come to his defense and rescue, from that day forward, he and his descendants would never sacrifice buffalos at funerals. He also made sure that his posterities understood and kept that covenant he had made with the buffalos. Thus buffalo sacrifice at funerals has been religiously forbidden to this day.

It is against this backdrop that Hmong migrated southward from central China and eventually reached Burma, Laos and Vietnam. My ancestors migrated to Laos from China through North Vietnam in the early 1800s. According to oral stories told us by my uncle Paaj Ceeb, who passed away March 7, 2011, great great grandpa Num Vwg left China and headed south to settle in northwestern Vietnam and northeastern Laos. Why did he leave China? Like many Hmong and other minority groups in China in the early 1800s, Num Vwg wanted a better life for his family that would be free from Chinese oppression and enslavement.

Num Vwg, or Muas Num Vwg (as he was known by and common in Hmong culture until recently) was a well-to-do family man. People in the community respected him and his leadership. Muas Num Vwg had two sons: Tsaav Toov and Suav Lauv. Tsaav Toov was my great grandfather.

As Tsaav Toov started his family, he became successful in his endeavors and was respected in the community. Because of his status in the community, he prepared an elaborate wedding reception for his eldest son Npla Kawm (who was my grandfather). As was early Hmong marriage tradition, there was a period of engagement before the wedding. As the wedding day approached, the groom's family would prepare an elaborate celebration as a reception for the bride and her family as she was being escorted to the groom's residence. Cooks and waiters were hired by the groom's family for this major event as was the case in those days. As a part of the wedding, alcohol (home-made, hard liquor) and other fermented drinks were readily available. People began to drink to their hearts' content. They were drunk and began a fight, and in the end, two of the chefs ended up dead – killing each other.

The result of this horrific event cost my great-grandfather and grandfather dearly. They lost, both socially and economically. They lost their respect and influence in the community. Economically, they lost their fortune. They were fined for the loss of two lives in the community. Spiritually, because Hmong believe the intertwining sphere between the physical and the spiritual, my great-grandfather and grandfather were "cursed". As such, my grandfather became very poor and my father became even poorer. My father became destitute so much so that he could not even afford to pay either of his wives' dowries (my father's first wife died not long after they had their first child, and my father remarried my mother some 10 years after his first wife's death).

I don't know much about my mother's family but remember vaguely about my maternal grandfather, Nkag Tswb Yaaj. Mom is the oldest of 10 kids. She and a sister, Ntxhoo, who is still in Laos, are the last two survivors of my grandfather's children. Three of her brothers died during the Vietnam conflict (the Secret War in Laos) in the 1960s. One brother and his wife passed away a few years ago in St. Paul, MN, and the last brother passed away in Laos three years ago. One of my aunts passed away a couple of years ago in North Vietnam. According to Mom, her biological mother passed away awhile back. The grandmother I knew was actually my real grandmother's sister, who had become widowed. When my grandfather became a widow, he married this sister-in-law so that she would become sort of a surrogate mother for my mother and her siblings.

In the late 1960s (probably 1967, 1968) I recall visiting my grandfather in their village, Tham Nee, on several occasions. On one occasion it was during peach ripening season. My brother Num Huas and I climbed my grandfather's peach trees to pick the ripened peaches. I also recall enjoying playing in the backyard or listening to grandpa telling fairy tale stories.

That was the last time I recall my maternal grandfather. Soon after that visit to my grand-father, our village and other nearby towns were invaded by Communist troops. We were chased out, never to return to normalcy again. He died from old age and natural causes in 1969. He was a good man, good father and grandfather to us, to me especially. My grandfather Nkag Tswb was also respected in his community. He was one of those men who was self-taught to read and write Lao. He became a village chief because of his ability to read and write Lao and also his innate leadership skills in dealing with village issues.

Son Cheng and his wife Aong

Daughters: From left – Pa Houa, Hli, and Hnou

Daughter Hnou and her husband Chris Gonzalez with Amelia Joy

Son Joshua and his wife Crystal

CHAPTER ONE

The birth of a child is a joyous occasion because it's the beginning of a new life, an addition to the family and the hope of a future uninterrupted. In literate and technologically advanced society, parents, with help of medical staff, make careful record of the weight and length of their new born babies and the time and date of their births. That was not the case with my parents however. They did not have the privileges that other advanced societies had. In Laos, there was no Hmong writing, and my parents and grandparents were illiterate. When I was born, there was no conventional healthcare system as in the industrialized nations. I was born in the home, and my father was my mother's "nurse" and "midwife" as was the case with all my siblings. Up until the fall of Laos and Vietnam in 1975, no one bothered to think of the importance of keeping any birth records.

And so, I don't know exactly when I was born, but I think it may have been in 1963. My mother told me I was born during rice harvest season, which is between late October and early November in the village of Nakaneng. My parents moved with other relatives and settled in Ban Phou Huard when I was six months old. This village was situated northeast of the military center Mueong Mok. It was here that I spent my first 7 or 8 years and began to make sense of life. I started to learn about my chores as a boy: feeding chickens, fending off neighbors' pigs during feeding time both early morning and before dusk, gathering hay for the family horse and my brother's fighting bull, and, of course, babysitting my nephews (Neeb and Yag) and accompanying my sister-in-law to the farm. I started school also in Ban Phou Huard, and it was here in this village that my father passed away when I was only 3 years old.

I don't remember very much about my father except for three experiences. One day my mother and my older brothers were working on the farm, and my father and I were home. As the sun was setting and Dad and I sat on the front porch waiting for Mom and the brothers to come home, he stroked the hair on my head back and forth and whispered into my ears: "One day Daddy will be no more, and my baby boy will be left an orphan." I recalled as Dad whispered these words to my ears that I would sob and sob. My sobbing stirred Dad's emotion greatly, and he started to cry. The two of us –father and son – would cry on each other's shoulders about the thought of losing one another.

The second occasion I recall about my father was after he had already died. I remember his body lying on the floor motionless; everyone else was mourning, and new clothes were put on his body in preparation for the funeral as I peeked over Mom's shoulders. It was a time of confusion for me because I did not know what was going on. I did not know why my dad would lie on the floor and not get up.

The third memory I have was the day he was to be buried. I remember being on my Mom's back as she mourned over Dad's body, which was starting to decompose.

In those days, there were no premade caskets to conceal the body nor balm to minimize and slow the decomposition of the body. In Hmong culture, people were not permitted to discuss death and anything associated with it, such as making funeral arrangements. To do so was taboo and continues to be in traditional Hmong culture even today. Hmong people are ingrained with the belief that planning for one's own last days (such as will-writing, funeral planning, selecting one's memorial and/or funeral services) would hasten the reality of death. It was such crippling fear that has been ingrained into Hmong culture and still impacts the Diaspora Hmong world-wide. It was in that setting that I peeked over Mom's shoulders and saw Dad's motionless, and now starting- to-change, body.

People have asked me how my dad died. I don't know. Again, there was no conventional healthcare system and neither hospital nor clinics anywhere near the village. Based on descriptions my mother gave of my dad's symptoms, he may have died from kidney failure or gallstone infection/ stones (I personally experienced gallstone infection and surgery several years ago.).

One day not long after Dad passed away, Mother, my older

brother Num Huas and I traveled to another village. As we were walking along, we came upon a man of Laotian descent walking some distance walking toward us. .. We knew him to be Qham Mai, but my brother still pointed his finger at him and exclaimed, "Daddy's coming over there! Daddy's coming over there!" "No. That's not Daddy," I replied "That's Qham Mai." Of course, being the "smart" boy that I was, I immediately rebuked him for his mistaking Qham Mai for Dad. I told him that Dad had already died and the man coming toward us was only the Laotian Qham Mai to his embarrassment and disappointment.

Since then, we somehow knew our dad would never come back from anywhere. That day the sense of loss and being an orphan hit home in a real way and lodged deeply in both my brother's and my mind and heart , but I was sure this experience made more of an impact on my brother. The word (and the idea of) "Dad" or "Daddy" or "Father" faded away. We knew that life without Dad would be forever. Thus we grew up fatherless. It wasn't until I came to the knowledge of God through the Lord Jesus Christ that I came to the realization that even though my earthly, biological father may be no more, my Heavenly Father is still on the throne and is constantly watching over me.

How blessed are those whose parents are still alive and well! At times the presence of parents in one's life may be more of a nuisance and bothersome than a blessing. At times, their behaviors and actions may get on one's nerves because they may act as though they are attempting to direct one's life. But I can say from personal experience that a parent's intentions are never to hurt or harm their children in any way. We never know the importance of a father's role in our lives until he is no more. It's then we realize that nothing and no one in the world can replace a father.

It was at that point, also, that my brothers and I came to realize the importance of our mother in our lives. Being a single parent is not an easy thing. And in my mother's situation, the struggles were compounded because of the economic situation of the time. However, it was a promise Dad made to Mom on his deathbed that kept her going .Knowing his condition was deteriorating and death was imminent, he had said to her: "Koj nam, kuv tug mob nuav ces ntshe yuav yog toomtxhob hab hlau khu xwb txhale zoo. Koj ua sab ntev tu kuv cov tub os. Maab tsis khi dluav. Zeb tsis nas hau. Ib nub twg koj cov tub yuav ua koj txiv ces yuav tsis txomnyem lawm. Koj ua sab ntev tu wb cov mivnyuas ces nub twg koj muab nyaab rua puab taag es puab tsheej cuab ntseg yim lawm ces kuv le nreg paas quas tawv lug tog koj. Es koj le ua kuv ntej es le lawv koj qaab es wb le moog su os."

Translated, it means, "Honey, this sickness of mine can only be healed by the spade and the hoe. You be patient in caring for my boys. Vines will not choke their waists. Rocks will not push down on their heads. One day your boys will become your father; then you will not be destitute anymore. You be patient caring for our children until you find them wives, and their families are established; then I will come back, leaning on my cane for you, and you will walk before me and we will go to rest."

not with us, it would be better for us to commit suicide so that we would be no more since Mom and Dad were no more.

After Dad's passing, my two oldest brothers stepped in to take the lead in the family, and they became father figures for the rest of us.. My brothers learned very quickly that the only way to gain respect with relatives and the community was to work hard, have helping hands, and have a "soft strength[1]."My brothers worked very hard, from using their strong hands to fell trees in clearing the forest for rice fields, to having "soft-hearted" personalities, they quickly gained the respect of relatives and the community and became recognized for their obvious commanding leadership skills.

As the conflict between the Viet Cong and the Royal Lao government escalated and fighting became intensified close to our region on the eastern border with North Vietnam, my two older brothers were drafted into the CIA SGU (Central Intelligent Agency Special Guerilla Unit) and became very active in the conflicts in the region.

---

1   "Zug Muas" or "Soft Strength" in Hmong means to be flexible and available, one of the values in Hmong culture. When a man makes himself available for service to his neighbors and relatives, others' hearts are opened to understand him and see the contribution he is making to the betterment of the community. The saying is similar to today's volunteerism attitudes and values. Unfortunately in today's world – the post-modern world – self-centeredness has become the value of the day for most people. And whatever they do tends to center around self more than others.

My brother Tsaav was trained to be a Reconnaissance Specialist[2] and team leader, working side by side with the American Advisors in the region. I recall one occasion when Mom took me to visit him at his "headquarters" in Mueong Mok, the regional military center about 10 kilometers from our home, Phou Huard.

Each time Mom and I went to visit him at his "office" and I saw him mingle with his American counterparts in their duties and eating eggs and sausages for breakfast, I thought it was cool. By the way, I was introduced to the American Advisors only by their first names: Jim and John.

My brothers worked hard juggling between their duties as commanding officers in their units and being father figures in our home, making sure the rest of us stayed safe at home. Even in the midst of conflicts and impending invasion from the enemies, my brothers made sure that Mom and the rest of us were provided and cared for back home.

As they got married and started their families, children were born to them and I became their babysitter since I was the youngest and had no other obligations as yet. I started babysitting Neeb and then Yag, and then Kaying and then Tub.

---

2   Merriam-Webster Dictionary defines reconnaissance as "a preliminary survey to gain information; especially an exploratory military survey of enemy territory." One of my brother's jobs was to work with the American advisors to determine enemy movements and strategize to thwart those movements.

TWO SOLDIERS CAME AND ANNOUNCED THAT MY BROTHER HAD BEEN KILLED...

It was April 1969. The sounds of bombs and canons could be heard from some distance away. As kids, we had been told to always be ready to leave the village because the communists could come at any time. And then, the sounds of bombs and canons became intensified and closer to home. Thus began the life of a refugee. We began the evacuation from the villages and moved to the open fields. Then, from there we were led to Pak Sahn by foot, and then by canoes through the Pak Sahn River to the city of Mueong Kao.

After spending a couple of weeks on the run, we reached Mueong Kao. I don't remember much about this trek into Mueong Kao, though. The next thing I remember was we were on our way "back home" because of terrible experiences people had during the refugee journey from home to Mueong Kao. People were dying. Young and old. From diseases and starvation and enemy attacks. So back the way we came, we went. A couple of canoes were hired and our families were put in them and we started north-bound on the Pak Sahn River.

On our way "back home," we settled on a mountainside called "Sam Boon." Soon an airstrip was built and helicopters were landing. Military advisors and trainers were deployed, and more equipment and supplies were dropped. Food supplies were provided for refugees. A new round of military training readied soldiers to make another offensive attempt to retake Mueong Mok. Sure enough. Home was "liberated," and we were encouraged to return a few months later after a moderate fire engagement with the enemy. My bother Tsaav had been in the frontline, with his comrades, making a constant push against the enemy, pushing them further away from the old military center, Mueong Mok, making it possible for us to return home. Life seemed to get back to normal again after a few months.

In August of 1969, Brother Tsaav led a team of half a dozen soldiers on a routine patrol into the surrounding area of the military center. He and his comrades encountered enemy troops and engaged the enemies in a firefight. After the attack, my brother and his soldiers fled from the enemy firing line. As they ran through an open area in a ravine, the enemy fired an RPG[3] rocket after my brother and his comrades. The rocket exploded as it landed on my brother's right shoulder, tearing his upper body, including his right hand and head. He was killed instantly. His surviving comrades came back to the Center and reported him MIA (missing in action). At his commander's order, a search and recovery team was deployed. Sure enough. His body was recovered at the site of the firefight without his upper body, his head and right hand.

---

3   According to Google, the **RPG-7** is a widely-produced, portable, unguided, shoulder-launched, anti-tank rocket-propelled grenade.. Originally the RPG-7 (Ручной Противотанковый Гранатомёт - *Ruchnoy Protivotankovyy Granatomyot, Hand-held anti-tank grenade launcher*), was designed by the Union. The English-language term "RPG," meaning "rocket-propelled grenade", though frequently encountered and reasonably descriptive, is not based on a literal translation.

I vividly recall that day. It was about three or four o'clock in the afternoon. I was babysitting at home. Two soldiers came to the house and announced that my brother was missing in action and was feared dead. That just turned my world upside down. Because I was at an impressionable age, the announcement about my brother being missing in action made a lasting impact on me. My future would never be the same. My hope was dashed because he was a father figure to me. Without his leadership there seemed to be no hope. No direction. And no future.

Dad and brother Tsaav are not the only ones our family has lost. My step brother Txhaj Lis (from my father's first wife) joined the Viet Cong when he became disenchanted with the royal government troop which suspected him of harboring enemy troops. One day, Txhaj Lis and a distant relative were summoned to the military center for questioning. When they arrived at the center, the military personnel treated them as traitors to the government and attempted to execute them for treason. A prominent commander tried to execute the relative at point blank -- without any concrete evidence and/or trial. But the bullet missed. It shaved off the lobe of his right ear instead. Because of this experience with the royal government troop, Txhaj Lis deserted them, including us, his family, and fled to the Viet Cong. He joined their ranks and soon was killed by a booby trap set by government troops. I did not have any chance to get to know him as a big brother.

I have lost family members over the years to diseases, starvation, and accidents. In fact, in 1977, I lost five family members in that one year. We were hiding in the jungles of Nam Tek during our hideout from the Communist Regime in Laos. Two sisters-in-law died from lack of medical care, and two nephews and a niece died from starvation. In 2000, my brother Vaam Pov died as a result of a fall from his manufactured home in Menomonee, WI.

It was a clear, sunny, and warm winter day in January. I was sitting in my Family & Youth Advancement Services, Inc. (FYASI) office on Payne Avenue in St. Paul. The phone rang (as it usually did since we were serving the needs of the community). The voice on the other end of the line, though, was that of Brother Nyaj Hawj. He said, "I have just hung up the phone with Brother Vaam Pov's wife. She said Vaam Pov fell from his rooftop as he climbed down from cleaning off the snow, and he was seriously injured. He was transported to the hospital. We need to go right now."

At that moment, my world began to turn upside down. My heart sank to the soles of my feet. Our family had already lost two brothers. We cannot lose another! As we drove to Menomonee that day, I prayed…and prayed… "Lord, restore my brother. Comfort our family." We entered the hospital and were escorted to the ER where my brother was already put on a ventilator. I looked over and saw him lying on the stretcher being strapped on to the bed. His body was motionless, yet his moaning could be heard in the hallway. I reached my hand to touch his forehead and whispered to him but there was no response. Vaam Pov's wife, my sister-in-law, was crying and attempted to recount the events that led up to the accident earlier in the day.

T. Cher and his family celebrating a Tribute to Mom.
April 20, 1999, St. Paul, MN
From left – Num Huas and his wife; Vaam Pov and
his wife, Mom, Nyaj Hawj and his 2 wives, Nuj
Sua and his wife, Txhaj Cawv and his wife

I proceeded to ask the attending medical team about his condition and was told that his injury was too severe for them to treat in Menomonee. He would have to be airlifted to the hospital in Eau Claire, 20 miles away to the east. As the ER staff began to prep for my brother's airlift, we drove ahead to Eau Claire.

At the hospital in Eau Claire we spent the rest of day and night and the next day waiting… and waiting. Those 24 hours – 10 a.m., January 5 to 10 a.m. January 6 – were some of the longest hours in my life. After some eight hours of surgery, the surgeon called a family conference. The first words from her mouth were, "I'm sorry. We were not able to help your brother. His right shoulder was severely broken and his skull was severely fractured and damaged due to the height of the fall. Even if we could save your brother's life, he would have become vegetative for the rest of his life."

Brother Vaam Pov drew his last breath and died from the injury he sustained from the fall at approximately 10 a.m., January 6, 2000. Vaam Pov's death brought home a valuable lesson about life, love and relationship. As brothers, we took each other and each other's company for granted for the longest time. We never realized the fragility of life. We lived life as though we were invincible. Sure, we experienced death in the family before. We experienced loss and loneliness – through the war, the deaths of Dad, brother Txhaj Lis, brother Tsaav and other family members. Maybe I was too young to reflect on the impact of those tragedies. Maybe we were too busy trying to survive that we didn't have the time to think about the value of each other's presence in our lives.

Then came the death of Brother Nuj Sua in 2004. Nuj Sua was diagnosed with cancer. Though initially doctors did not know where the cancer root was, the disease was discovered on his liver, as he went to the hospital for complications of the kidneys. He was diagnosed with cancer in October, 2003, and died within six months. Shortly before his death, I took him to Mayo Clinic in Rochester, MN, and doctors there were able to tell us that he was at a very advanced stage of stomach cancer, and they could not do anything much to help. Brother Nuj Sua also expressed his wishes to not seek further treatment for this terroristic disease and spent his last days at home.

He died peacefully on the morning of May 11, 2004, at approximately 5 a.m. All of us who loved and cared about him were at his bedside when he passed into the presence of God. A couple of days before his death, though, as I looked at his frail and progressively deteriorating body, I could tell he was desperate to taste food, but his digestive system could not tolerate it because of the severe cancer in the stomach. Eventually he confided in me saying, "Oh. How I long to dine with Jesus in heaven. I am so looking forward to dining with the Lord Jesus in heaven." After he expressed this desire, his demeanor changed. He seemed to have a genuine yearning for his spirit to depart and be with Jesus. He seemed to have a longing with anticipation that his time to meet his Savior was imminent.

**Shortly before our departure to
Bangkok for America, 1979
From left – Nuj Sua, Brother-in-law Vam Xeeb Vwj, Num
Huas, sister Maiv Neeb, T. Cher and niece and nephews.**

Brother Nuj Sua's death impacted my life much more than I realized, probably because of the role he played in my life when I was younger. In May of 1977, when I was a young teenager, our family had been hiding, for two long years, in the jungles of Laos waiting and hoping in vain for the royal government to return and liberate the remnants of the former CIA Guerilla fighters. My brothers and others decided to ditch their plan of holding out for such false expectations, and they made plans for our family to make the long, treacherous and dangerous trek across mountains and ravines of Laos to Thailand.

After a two weeks' trek with at least four hundred other people including women and children, we made it to the top of Phou Ngu or Snake Mountain, overlooking the Mekong River down in the valley. We saw Thailand just over the horizon. We stood on the Snake Mountaintop looking over the sunset, and as the sun went down over the west, street lights began to light the night sky in Thailand. We longed for the day when we would cross the dark and dreadful jungles of Laos (where we had just come from) to a place dawning with endless possibilities for the future. All of us who gathered there on that mountain top were so hopeful. We hoped with a great sense of anticipation that, by dawn the next day, all would land safely in Thai soil. And we would taste freedom and liberty again, for the first time in a long, long time.

After two weeks of roaming the mountain top, risking all 400 plus lives, and making at least two failed trips to the Mekong Shore, brother Nuj Sua (then in his 20s) and another young man decided to ditch everyone else and risked their lives to cross the Mekong River to freedom in Thailand. Because Nuj Sua took this risk, he was able to return to Laos in August 1978 and help guide and protect the rest of the family as we made our trek across the same path from Laos to Thailand. In a word, Nuj Sua was instrumental in our family's safe passage from the jungles of Laos to freedom in Thailand and eventually resettlement and success in America.

He was a leader and a friend. After several years of separation between the two of us, my family and I were able to move to the Twin Cities where Nuj Sua was living. I became his and his family's pastor for several years. So at church and on Sunday, I was the pastor. Monday through Saturday, however, he was my big brother and friend. We went fishing together -- even to Devil's Lake in North Dakota. To save money on groceries, he and I would go to the slaughtering house and share half of a cow or pig. We raised our children together, our families camped together, we vacationed together, we did special activities together – he, his wife and children with my wife, children and me. Just our two families. We were not only brothers, we were also friends and companions. We even had a joint Janitorial Service business for a couple of years. Those were the days.

I WANTED TO BE A PILOT...

Whether we want to admit it or not, our thought processes, our ambitions in and for life, our behaviors and actions are impacted and shaped by our environment and significant people in our lives. Parents, teachers, politicians, movie stars, and others make huge impacts in our lives. For me, Ly Lue, a Hmong T-28 fighter pilot made a lasting impression on me. I grew up in the war, which influenced on my life tremendously. Ly Lue was one of the Hmong fighter pilots who flew a T-28 fighter jet during the peak of the conflict. As a kid, we heard a lot about Ly Lue and how heroic and daring he was as a patriotic pilot. Yes, there were a lot of other Hmong and Lao fighter pilots, but Ly Lue was the one everyone talked about. And even kids like us heard the adults talk about him and his flawless efforts at bombing his targets. So my ambition as a kid was to be a pilot.

So when I grew up I wanted to be a pilot. I wanted to be famous, like Mr. Ly Lue. But I also wanted to be a pilot because I felt that my country had been destroyed by enemies. I wanted to protect my home, my country. I wanted to prevent the enemy from coming and taking over my home country. That dream, however, faded after our land was invaded and our homes were taken over – by enemy troops – and we ended up roaming the jungles until the fall of Laos and Vietnam.

A part of being a kid is to have fun. Having fun back then, though, was not like that of today's children who have abundant manufactured toys. But we made due what we could and had a lot of fun by what we made. I remember playing with neighbor kids. Because we grew up in the war, our daily lives were influenced by the ideas of war including fighter jets, guns, grenades, and chutes. We learned to carve planes, guns, and other military figurines from wood we could cut or find.

Another fun and yet daring thing that I remember very vividly was riding down hills on banana tree trunks. Instead of using conventional toys and equipment, we cut ourselves good size banana tree trunks, punched holes through one end of the trunk, pushed a wooden stick through it, and fastened a rope on the two ends of the wooden stick as one would harness a horse. Then we would go up a steep hill and, from the top of the hill, we would use this "horse" to slide down!. We didn't realize how dangerous these activities were, but it sure was fun. Kids had fun. We didn't have a thing to worry about. That was the life of a kid at the time.

Up until 1967, there was no school in the vicinity. When a school opened and a teacher was sent to our village, I was one of the very first kids to enroll. When the time came for school registration, parents would take their children to school, and teachers and others would determine whether the kids were school-ready. A common way to determine a child's readiness for school was to ask the child to reach over his head and attempt to touch his opposite ear. If he could do that, then he was determined to be of school-age! Thus was the way I was admitted to school.

School back then was predominantly for boys. The belief was that girls were born for the family and the farm, while boys were born for the community and the country. Girls were to grow up and be industrious, working the farm with their hands and not with their minds, while boys were to grow up to be men of the community and serve the country.

I was ecstatic when I was able to go to school for the first time. As a young boy, I had a keen mind and was able to grasp the alphabets very quickly, even though the academics were in Lao (Hmong was not put into writing until the late 1940s/early 1950s by French and American missionaries). Very quickly I was able to memorize the Lao alphabet and became the teacher's "pet." Before long, our teacher, Mr. Ken, appointed me "Assistant Teacher," giving me the authority over my fellow students.

As the 1968-69 school-year arrived, I was able to attend the school at the military center, Mueong Mok, as a second grader. The only mode of transportation for us at the time was by foot. I remember walking to school every morning with my cousins, which took us at least a couple of hours each way. On the way to school we had to pass two Lao villages – Ban Mueong Mok and Qham Vieng – and several rice paddies. In those rice paddies, especially during March and April when the rice was already being harvested and the land was furloughed until the next farming season, were lots of water buffaloes grazing through the leftover rice stalks and grass on the fields. As kids, we had had little contact with buffaloes; we were scared of those humongous creatures – at least they were huge in the eyes of the beholders – us kids!

I remember on one occasion when we were on our way home from school, we came upon a herd of buffaloes with a huge bull standing in front of all the others – about 20 or 30 of them grazing grass, and they were blocking our pathway home. He was staring right at us home-bound school kids as if to say: "You are not coming through this way. If you kids are going to go pass this way, you will have to come through me!" And he seemed to be very serious about it, too.

So, instead of going back the way we came earlier in the day, we took a detour – a very long and prickly detour – away from the buffalo herd and into the jungle on the north side of the rice paddies. It took twice as long that day to get home than the usual every day trip. Talk about being scared! That was one of the scariest and most memorable moments of my childhood.

Mai Yia, Nam Kx. Paj Txhim Muas, and Niam Kx. Nyiaj Kaub Lauj pose in front of a Hmong Tsevteb (Ricefi eld Hut), outside of Ban Hoi Han, Chiang Rai, Th ailand, 1997.

Chapter Two

I vividly remember April of 1969, even though I was probably only about six years old. The sounds of bombs, grenades, and canons could be heard from some distance away. We were told that Communist troops were closing in on nearby villages, and a military center was lost to Communist hands. We also were told to leave our village and move into the fields to the southwest. For the adults, this was a heartbreaking point. My mother and brothers had to release all of their livestock – cattle, horses, goats, pigs, and chickens. What the villagers left behind was more than just their animals and their bamboo-roofed or wooden-roofed houses. They left behind their lives, their community, their identities. They had become refugees in their own villages and eventually their country. But for us kids, moving was fun despite having to leave home and school. We got to sleep outdoors and gaze at the stars at night without any tents or covers. We would just sleep with friends in the open fields. Those were the fun days.

We left the village, never to return home, just as Scar would tell Simba in the movie, The Lion King: "Leave Pride Rock and never return." Since the day we left our village, Ban Phu Huard, we roamed the countryside until 1975, except for a brief half a month when we returned to have just enough time for my brother to give his life for his country, and for us, his family, to bury his body. Then in1976, we started roaming again until 1978. In a way, we roamed the jungles of Laos for almost ten years.

After we buried Brother Tsaav in Meuong Mok in September, 1969, my brother Nyaj Hawj decided to separate from the rest of the relatives and move away on a three days' journey to the south. In 1970, our family settled in the outskirts of a recently established village, Nam Kou, which had been established by my deceased brother Tsaav's in-laws. They had sufficient rice for themselves and were able to share with others. We were the beneficiaries of their bountifulness and benevolence. That year, 1970, as my widowed sister-in-law's uncle's rice field ripened, we were invited to harvest the first crop with him. Thus, we were spared from starvation.

I learned later that the majority of the American public knew little or nothing about the conflict in Laos. When it came to the conflict in Asia, Vietnam came into mind after the Korean War. But Laos? No one knew. It was a surprise to the American public that the U.S. government supported such a conflict concurrently with the Vietnam conflict. It is known as the Secret War because the U.S. government, under Presidents John F. Kennedy, Lyndon Johnson, Richard Nixon, and Gerald Ford had kept U.S. involvement a secret.

Politically, in the eyes of the world, the kingdom of Laos was neutral in Southeast Asia. It was believed that there may have been internal conflicts between different political factions, but never full-blown warfare in Laos. Secretly, though, the U.S. government, through the CIA, supported the Royal Lao government and a ragtag people group known back then as the Miao. But we called ourselves Hmong.

The following Wikipedia article describes in detail the conflict in Laos from 1945 through the fall of Vietnam in 1975, including the involvement of other world powers such as the U.S. This article will help clarify the misunderstandings and misconceptions surrounding the influx of Hmong, Lao, Cambodian and Vietnamese refugees into Third-world countries and the United States.

> Between 1964 and 1968 the conflict in Laos was essentially between the U.S.-supported government forces and the Pathēt Lao, supplied by Vietnam. The Pathēt Lao in these years was not a real threat to the government. The real problem for the government was corruption and warlordism within the national army. Regional army commanders did not cooperate with each other effectively and spent more time on political maneuvers than on fighting the Pathēt Lao. Suvannaphūmā's government was an unwilling prisoner of events. Suvannaphūmā continued to argue for a neutralised Laos, and both sides paid lip-service to this ideal, but neither was prepared to yield any part of its strategic position to achieve it. In particular, the North Vietnamese had

no intention of withdrawing any part of their army from the areas of the country it occupied.

Suvannaphūmā remained in office, despite frequent threats to resign, because both the U.S. and the North Vietnamese preferred him to anyone else. The U.S. no longer bothered opposing his neutralist views because, as the paymasters of the Lao army, they could ignore him and conduct the war as they saw fit. The North Vietnamese on the other hand didn't really consider Laos an independent country. They considered it an underdeveloped region of their empire that needed their guidance. As in Cambodia, as long as neutralism meant the departure of the Americans and left the North Vietnamese army in the territories it controlled, they favoured it.

In 1968 the North Vietnamese army pushed the Pathēt Lao forces aside and took over the fighting of the war. In January North Vietnam sent its 316th Division forward toward the Nambac Valley, where seven of the government's best military units were located. The valley was surrounded and pounded with artillery until the base eventually fell. The battle effectively ended the role of the Royal Lao Army for the next several years. While the Pathēt Lao were an ineffective force, the North Vietnamese army with its Soviet-provided field artillery and tanks was beyond anything that the Lao Army could deal with. The government disbanded all its forces greater than the size of a battalion and disengaged from the conflict.

Between 1968 and 1973 Laos effectively ceased to exist as an independent state. It became a battlefield in the war between the United States and North Vietnam. The Hmong militias and Thai Army forces, on one side, and the North Vietnamese Army with the assistance of the Pathēt Lao, on the other, were engaged as auxiliary fighters. The country was divided into two zones: one - comprising about two-thirds of Laos but containing only about a quarter of its population - effectively controlled by North Vietnam, and the other - consisting of little more than the Mekong Valley but containing most of the Lao population - effectively controlled by the U.S. The Pathēt Lao, for reasons discussed earlier, were willing collaborators in the Vietnamese control of their zone of operations. They knew that the only way they could hope to take power in Laos was via the power of the North Vietnamese. While it is often said that Laos was a vital supply route for North Vietnam, the reality was not quite so tidy. Portions of Southern Laos were useful to North Vietnam, but North Vietnam occupied large sections of the country that had nothing to do with supply routes.

The U.S. objective in Laos was to push government control as far eastward as practical. It sought to prevent the North Vietnamese and Pathēt Lao forces holding the Plain of Jars. After 1968, the US accomplished this mainly through Vang Pao's Hmong militia. The other U.S. objectives were intelligence gathering and interruption of North Vietnam's use of the Ho Chi

Minh trail, and for this it relied on air power. During this period Laos was bombed more heavily than any other country ever has been in history: virtually every town and village in the Pathēt Lao zone was destroyed and most of the population made refugees. The North Vietnamese objectives were more complicated. Their primary goal was to keep the Ho Chi Minh trail in the south open, and to prevent the U.S. using Laos as a base for raids into North Vietnam. The war degenerated into the two sides pushing each other into or out of the Plain of Jars.

In 1969 Richard Nixon became President of the U.S. and began the long process of winding down the Vietnam War and finding a political settlement. But this brought no immediate respite in Laos. The new administration pursued the same goals by the same means, and in fact during 1969 and 1970 the bombing campaign increased in intensity. The extension of the war to Cambodia in 1970, which closed North Vietnam's supply routes through that country, made the Ho Chi Minh trail even more crucial to the course of the Vietnam War. In the spring of 1969 the North Vietnamese attempted to hold the Plain of Jars through the rainy season. This led to a coordinated campaign which led to a disastrous defeat of the North Vietnamese. Under constant pressure, their resistance collapsed in the Plain of Jars. They abandoned millions of dollars worth of military equipment and were chased almost to the North Vietnamese border. The success however was short-lived. The North Vietnamese launched a two-division counteroffensive led by a large tank force. All the gains of that year were lost back to the North Vietnamese.

In March 1970 the Cambodian government of Lon Nol ended the policy of ignoring the Vietnamese presence in the country. The port of Sihanoukville in Cambodia, which had effectively been a North Vietnamese Army supply terminal for years, was closed by the government. This action had the effect of making the supply routes from North Vietnam through Laos even more important to the North Vietnamese. In the spring of 1970 the North Vietnamese Army began advancing westward deeper into Laos than ever before. During the same year, units of the Thai Army entered the conflict. These so-called Unity Battalions were in theory volunteers, but were effectively Thai regulars.

In 1971 the Royal Lao Army came back into the conflict. The North Vietnamese advance deep into the country destroyed the status quo and prompted the Army back into action. In July the Thai and irregular forces attempted a repeat of the successful 1969 offensive into the Plain of Jars. But the North Vietnamese had learned from their previous mistakes and withdrew in good order ahead of the offensive. While much territory was captured, no serious damage was done to the North Vietnamese Army. The Thai and irregular forces built a chain of fortifications down the middle of the Plain of Jars. In 1971 the U.S. sponsored an invasion of southern Laos by the South Vietnamese army, with the aim of severing the trail and shoring up the South Vietnamese government as the U.S. withdrew its combat troops. The invasion was bitterly resisted by North Vietnamese and was decisively defeated. The North Vietnamese also retaliated by capturing several provincial capitals which it had previously surrounded but not tried to take.

An estimated 200,000 people were killed in Laos in the course of the war, most of them Lao civilians. While the ethnic minorities who mainly populated the mountains of the Pathēt Lao suffered terribly as a result of the U.S. air war, the majority of the Lao-Lum people in the Mekong Valley towns were little affected in a military sense. The influx of U.S. personnel and money (an estimated $US500 million in U.S. aid alone) produced an economic boom in the towns as service industries grew to meet the demands of the war and the large resident American civilian population. Lao generals and politicians, led by Phūmī Nôsavan until his fall from power in 1965, grew rich on corruption, drug dealing, prostitution and smuggling, and large numbers of ordinary Lao moved into the cash economy for the first time, particularly in Viang Chan, which grew rapidly. The war also exposed the Lao to the full force of western popular culture for the first time, with an effect that both the Pathēt Lao and conservative Buddhists regarded as deeply corrupting of Lao tradition and culture.

During these years the Pathēt Lao sought to project an image of moderation both domestically and internationally. Suphānuvong, as head of the Lao Patriotic Front, was the public face of the Pathēt Lao, while the Communist Party and its leader Kaisôn remained in the background. At its 1968 congress, the Front issued a 12-point program which made no mention of socialism, but called for a Government of National Union and free elections, and promised respect for Buddhism and the monarchy. The fact that Suphānuvong was a royal prince as well as a communist seemed to many Lao a reassurance that the Pathēt Lao in power would pursue a moderate path. In the Pathēt Lao zone, the communists followed conspicuously moderate policies, although there were some attempts at collectivising agriculture where this was possible. The Pathēt Lao were effective providers of basic services, despite the difficulties created by the endless bombing, and also effective at mobilising the upland minorities, whom they treated with far greater respect than any Lao government had ever done. Most notably, the Pathēt Lao were free from corruption. On the negative side, as most Lao knew, their policies were largely driven by the North Vietnamese.

In January 1973, following Nixon's re-election, a peace agreement was announced between North Vietnam and the U.S. Following the pattern which had been established in Geneva in 1954, a peace settlement in Laos was agreed on as a side issue to the Vietnam question. The two sides in Laos had been in informal discussions since the previous July, and once their respective patrons had consented, they quickly signed a ceasefire and announced an Agreement on the Restoration of Peace and National Reconciliation. The main provisions were the formation of a Third Coalition government, with Suvannaphūmā as prime minister and 12 ministers from each side. The National Assembly, which had long lost its political legitimacy, was to be replaced by a Consultative Council of 42 members - 16 from each side plus ten agreed nominees. This body, to be chaired by Suphānuvong, was given equal status with the government, making Suphānuvong in effect co-ruler of the country.

There was no mention of the Pathēt Lao giving up *de facto* control of its zone. Its armed forces were to be integrated into the national army in theory, but the timetable was never really certain. While the agreement required the North Vietnamese Army to leave Laos, the Vietnamese never left. The arrangements reflected the vastly strengthened position of the Pathēt Lao since the Second Coalition government. In recognition of this, the rightists attempted a last-gasp *coup* in Viang Chan in August, but it quickly collapsed, since by then many Lao recognised that it was only a matter of time before the Pathēt Lao took power.

During 1974 and 1975 the balance of power in Laos shifted steadily in favour of the Pathēt Lao as the U.S. disengaged itself from Indochina. Suvannaphūmā was tired and demoralised, and following a heart attack in mid 1974 he spent some months recuperating in France, after which he announced that he would retire from politics following the elections scheduled for early 1976. The anti-communist forces were thus leaderless, and also divided and deeply mired in corruption. Suphānuvong, by contrast, was confident and a master political tactician, and had behind him the disciplined cadres of the communist party and the Pathēt Lao forces and the North Vietnamese army. The end of American aid also meant the mass demobilization of most of the non-Pathēt Lao military forces in the country. The Pathēt Lao on the other hand continued to be both funded and equipped by North Vietnam. In May 1974 Suphānuvong put forward an 18-point plan for "National Reconstruction," which was unanimously adopted - a sign of his increasing dominance. The plan was mostly uncontroversial, with renewed promises of free elections, democratic rights and respect for religion, as well as constructive economic policies. But press censorship was introduced in the name of "national unity," making it more difficult for non-communist forces to organise politically in response to the creeping Pathēt Lao takeover. In January 1975 all public meetings and demonstrations were banned. Recognising the trend of events, influential business and political figures began to move their assets, and in some cases themselves, to Thailand, France or the U.S.

In 1975, the Pathēt Lao forces on the Plain of Jars supported by North Vietnamese heavy artillery and other units began advancing westward. In late April, the Pathēt Lao took the government outpost at Sala

Phou Khoum crossroads which opened up Route 13 to a Pathēt Lao advance toward Muang Kassy. For the non-Pathēt Lao elements in the government, compromise seemed better than allowing what had happened in Cambodia and South Vietnam to happen in Laos. A surrender was thought to be better than a change of power by force.[4]

In 2002, Jeff Lindsay of Appleton, WI, wrote the following essay describing Hmong involvement with the U.S.'s Secret War in Laos, which was published in *FutureHmong* Magazine. Here's what he had to say:

In the late 1950s, Southeast Asia, including Laos, was viewed as an important region to the West. With the fall of China to communism and the rise of Communist rebellion in Vietnam, the US sent elite soldiers, the Green Berets, to train Hmong guerrillas to oppose the Vietnamese and the Pathet Lao communists of Laos. Though the Hmong had no desire to play political roles for other nations, they loved freedom and know that there would be little freedom under Communism. They were threatened by the intrusion of North Vietnamese troops into Laos, so the U.S. then encouraged them to fight and provided training and weapons. With CIA assistance, General Vang Pao became the leader of a secret army of 9,000 Hmong men in 1961. Laos was officially neutral as the Vietnam War broke out, and the US had signed an international agreement, the Geneva Accords, intended to keep Laos neutral and

---

4   Reprinted by permission from Wikipedia.

prevent fighting there. In reality, this agreement gave the Communists the upper hand, for they flagrantly violated the agreement. Responding to the presence of active North Vietnamese troops in Laos, the US tried to oppose them without appearing to violate the Geneva Accords by secretly recruiting freedom-loving locals to fight the Communist -- and these freedom-loving locals were the Hmong.

Most Americans thought that Laos was not part of the Vietnam War, but Laos played a critical role, especially since supplies from North Vietnam to its warring troops primarily moved along the Ho Chi Minh trail that passed through Laos. Much fighting occurred along this trail and the surrounding regions in Laos. But our military efforts there were not publicized to avoid international criticism. So we pretended that nothing was happening in Laos, while North Vietnamese troops were actively helping the Pathet Lao take over the country, and while thousands of poorly-equipped Hmong were fighting a war against terrible odds. Many Hmong lives would be lost in the unpublicized battles of Laos.

The Hmong apparently were told that they could bravely fight for the U.S. because the United States would always be there to protect them should local communists turn on the Hmong. It was a relationship of trust, but Hmong trust in the US would be sadly misplaced.

In 1963 the Kennedy Administration had the CIA

increase the secret Hmong army in Laos to 20,000 soldiers. Significant battles occurred as the North Vietnamese and Pathet Lao occupied major areas in northern Laos in 1964. Meanwhile, the US began a secret air war in Laos. By 1968, US pilots would be doing 300 dangerous sorties a day to battle many thousands of Communist troops. Hmong soldiers rescued many American pilots who were shot down. Sometimes dozens of Hmong would die in order to rescue one American pilot. Over 100 Hmong pilots were recruited and trained by the US, and they ran mission after mission until they were all killed. Hmong courage seemed to know no bounds in the fight for freedom. But sadly, much of the fighting seems to have been in vain.

Years after the war, when the infamous "Pentagon Papers" were published, shocked Americans and Hmong patriots would learn that much of the war was fought by the United States under secret rules that we agreed to that almost guaranteed the fall of South Vietnam to the Communists. Just as the Hmong were told to only fight defensively and not to take steps that could directly throw the North Vietnamese out of their country, so too were U.S. actions continually hampered by rules of engagement, apparently orchestrated by Robert S. McNamara, the US Secretary of Defense at the time. For example, US pilots were not allowed to attack Viet Cong anti-aircraft installations until they were fully functional. Though hotly debated, many are convinced that the war could have been won by cutting off supplies to the North Vietnamese and hitting them in the regions where they were most vulnerable -- something that was forbidden by our rules of engagement. Instead, American soldiers died unnecessarily in jungle skirmishes that gave an upper hand to those familiar with the territory.

The loss of 60,000 American lives for a no-win war in Vietnam was a tragedy to the huge nation of America, but it was a relatively small percentage of the nation compared to the loss the Hmong people suffered. In 1969, at the time when Congress first learned of our secret war in Laos, about 18,000 Hmong soldiers had already been killed in battle and many women and children had died as well. The Hmong were taking a great risk in boldly fighting for the United States, trusting that we would stand by them. But in 1973, the U.S. began to pull out of Laos, leaving the Hmong on their own to fight thousands of North Vietnamese troops in Laos. By 1975, Laos had fallen completely into Communist hands, and the lives of all Hmong people who helped fight the Communists were in jeopardy. More than 100,000 Hmong fled to Thai refugee camps. Many would be killed along the way, especially when crossing the Mekong River to get to Thailand. An estimated 30,000 Hmong would be killed by Communist forces while trying to reach Thailand. Over 100,000 Hmong ... died as a result of the war, and today nearly every Hmong family in the US has terrible tales of loss and tragedy relating to the war.

The United States, recognizing the sacrifice made by Hmong soldiers to fight for the U.S., began accepting Hmong refugees into the United States in December of 1975. By 1990, about 100,000 refugees had entered the United States. Today approximately 250,000 Hmong are in the U. S, and a similar number still live in Laos.[5]

As was the case with most of the Hmong, my family was drawn into the conflict. My brothers had no choice but to join the Special Guerrilla Unit (SGU) army to defend our borders from invading enemies. After the U.S. pulled out of the conflict in 1975, the leadership that was involved with the CIA and their inner circle of personnel were airlifted to Thailand. The rest of us were left to fend for ourselves. But instead of bowing to the Communist government, my family, like most of the former CIA-affiliated officers, fled to the jungles, picking up the CIA-era left-over weapons on the way. We resisted the Communist regime, hoping for the Royal Laos Government to return and restore freedom and liberty as in former days.

As a kid, I never understood why there was fighting and never understood why we had to leave our village. Now, as I look back and I read the arguments from all sides -- the Communist side, the Royal Government side, and the CIA side -- and talk to people who were directly involved in the conflict, I think it was a mistake on all sides. I say to people

5   Essay by Jeff Lindsay, Appleton, Wisconsin. (Published in FutureHmong Magazine, June 2002, pp. 14-15.)

I know that the U.S. could have won the war if they had simply decided to win the war. But for some reason, the U.S. decided to pull out of Vietnam and Southeast Asia. In the end, governments involved may come to realize that those conflicts were not worth fighting for.

Behind the scenes, maybe there were political reasons for the conflict. A few years ago, I went to Thailand and visited a Hmong village where I met a man who had fled Laos to Thailand. But before fleeing to Thailand, he had been involved with the Communists. He shared with me that in 1975, especially in Laos, the Communist insurgents were on the verge of losing the battle because there was nobody back in the headquarters; every soldier was deployed to the capital. "If you guys knew," he said, "you could have taken the whole country and that would have been the end of it. But you didn't do it."

I thought, "Man, that is interesting! Now you have revealed the secret behind the secret." I believed the war was a waste of life, resources, time, and a waste of relationships. Looking back, there may have been political reasons for those involved to pull out. But for us and for me, I feel that the U.S. could have won the war in Southeast Asia. Instead it chose to abandon Laos, Cambodia and Vietnam to fend for themselves – especially those who were being trained to fight with and for the U.S.' CIA.

⌒⤨⌒

We never stayed in a place longer than two or three years at a time once we fled our village in April 1969. One of the most difficult and life altering experiences for a young boy was to care for kids who were not your own, and yet you have no choice but care for them while you yourself have no hope, no future, and no direction. Besides being constantly on the move, from one jungle to the next and one mountain to the next, I became the surrogate father to my two orphaned nephews, the sons of my oldest brother Tsaav who had been killed in action.

When Tsaav died, my second oldest brother, Nyaj Hawj, became the leader, father figure, and provider for us during our time of roaming. He became to me a friend and a leader, especially during the time when we were roaming the jungles because we were the "team of two" who provided for the family as far as food and shelter were concerned. Brother Nyaj Hawj and I were the main hunters and food foragers for a family of 13 people throughout 1977 and 1978, until we made it safely to Thailand.

FORAGING WHATEVER WAS EDIBLE TO SURVIVE...

To survive as a refugee in one's own country, a person has to be "creative," including being a "smart thief." Let me explain. During the rice harvest season in 1977, Communist troops occupied our village, Phu Ma Thao, and the surrounding area. We were hiding as bandits in the jungles nearby. Food was becoming more and more scarce, and we became more and more desperate. The rice fields were turning yellow, a sign that the fields were ripe for harvest. There was, however, one major problem. With air power and superior weapons, the enemy troops controlling the villages and patrolling the surrounding rice fields, made it impossible to harvest those crops. We, on the other hand, were a small band of former CIA-trained and backed Guerrilla officers, along with their helpless, hopeless, directionless, and futureless families with small children. But we also had CIA-era leftover and outdated small weaponry and equipment.

To avoid and minimize direct confrontation with enemy troops, we would forage roots, fruits, and any wild rattan and palm hearts available. In essence, in order to survive, we foraged whatever was edible. But then, it was necessary to go back and "harvest" the rice from the fields. But harvesting rice from the rice fields was not a simple task. We became "thieves" in our own rice fields. We became "Rats," sneaking in on our fields at dusk, gleaning rice stalks from the farthest edges of the fields, from dusk 'til dawn, and hiding them as far away from potentially dangerous areas of enemy troops.

I CARRIED A GUN BY THE TIME I WAS 13 OR 14…

Because of the confusion when the communists invaded our region, there was a period of time– about three months – during which my brother Vaam Pov, his wife and child, Num Huas, one of my orphaned nephews, Tub, and I got separated from the rest of the family. We roamed the jungles, staying a few days here and a few days there before moving again. I had my backpack full of a few personal belongings and enough food for a few days, and on top of it was a "saddle" for nephew Tub because he was too young and too sick to walk on his own in the thick and rugged jungles. I would carry him on my shoulders. Plus, I had to carry a gun for protection on our journey. (I was exposed to weapons of war at a very early age. I carried a gun by the time I was thirteen or fourteen. Not just for fun or for games, but for protection against the imminent enemy threat.) The gun I carried was an M-1. It was a semi-automatic and its magazine holds 8 bullets. At times the gun seemed to be an extra burden when a person carried so much, not only physically, but mentally and psychologically. But for personal safety and community protection, it was necessary, especially during times of conflict and you were on the run from your enemies. I carried that gun to protect myself, my family, and others who were on the journey with us. Those were some of the most difficult times in my life as a refugee in Laos.

We eventually decided to leave the country...

After three years in the jungle, eating roots and leaves and fruit trees with a lot of people dying from starvation and malnutrition and lack of medical treatment since the fall of Vietnam, Laos and Cambodia, we decided to leave the country. Few people back then, especially young people like me, realized, the day you step out of your country (especially by force), that it would be the last to call it your own. You would become a refugee or an immigrant. We decided in 1977 at harvest time to cross the rugged mountains and then swim the Mekong river to get from Laos to Thailand. On our first attempt, we were unable to cross the river. My brother, Nuj Sua, decided that he was no longer able to stay behind. He wanted to move ahead. He swam across the Mekong River while being shot at by Communist troops from the shores.

We went back to the jungle and spent another year there. In September of 1978, during the harvest of the first crop, my brother, came back with plastic swimming tubes for us to use as swimming aides to cross the Mekong River. I remember very vividly September 22, 1978. After a ten-day trip from the jungles through rugged mountains and steep valleys, we came to the border of Laos and Thailand. On the horizon the sun was setting and as the evening began, we could see street lights in Thailand begin to light up the darkening skies. But around and behind us was darkness. Darkness so thick that one could feel and almost touch it.

Beyond the Mekong River lay freedom, liberty, and peace. Just beyond the River, there were opportunities to live in peace and to pursue one's dreams and passion. But crossing the Mekong was more than crossing a physical barrier between two countries. It was about crossing from war to peace. From being hunted as wild animals to being able to live as human beings in community. From oppression to freedom. Essentially, from death to life. But we didn't realize the price we would end up paying – becoming refugees in a foreign land and never returning to the land of our births. There were about four hundred or more people in our group.

September is the monsoon season. That meant that torrential rains were constant on most days. The forest floors were drenched. And so were we. Streams and rivers were at full flood stage. The Mekong River is not only a major body of water stretching Laos from north to south, but also serves as a border between Laos and Thailand. The Mekong River was thus the dividing line between both countries. The monsoon season compounded and complicated the barrier between Laos and Thailand.

As we reached the Mekong River shores and prepared to cross over, canoes that my brother Nuj Sua and his teammates had hired arrived. Children and the elderly were being transported to Thailand without much problem. The rest of the people, though, had no choice but to swim with the help of fresh-cut bamboo logs we brought along to use as floating devices. There were six of us in our family who had to resort to swimming, myself included.

At nine o'clock at night on September 22, we plunged into the Mekong water and started swimming without any second thoughts about potential slithering snakes and/or other who-knows-what objects floating downstream. In order to minimize a potential loss of life in the journey, we paired two people together by tying ropes on each other's waists. Brother Nyaj Hawj and his son Yag, were tied as a pair; Brother Vaam Pov and sister-in-law, Tsaav's widow, were a second pair. My niece, Ntxhi and I were tied as the third pair.

As we started swimming against the Mekong currents, I realized that my strength began to weaken. My chest began to hurt. I soon realized I may not make it to Thailand. And

I may not have the opportunity to see freedom and pursue the dreams I had thus far. Then I called to my brothers and asked them to wait for me and my niece. The response was, "Just come along. We will wait for you." But they did not. Of course, they could not, because of the fast and furious monsoon currents of the Mekong River.

I DIDN'T KNOW HOW MANY MORE MINUTES I COULD SURVIVE…

So that left my niece and me to our own fate. A mile south of where we started swimming, there was a smaller body of water, Nam Kading or the Kading River, which intersected with the Mekong River. The intersection formed a whirlpool.

As my niece Ntxhi and I were floating and drifting downstream, we were sucked into this whirlpool. We tried to swim but mostly swirled around in that whirlpool from nine o'clock that night to four or five o'clock the next morning. As we struggled for survival and life, we didn't know if we were going to make it. Death seemed imminent. My niece and I were two helpless and hopeless souls in the midst of a vast, fast, furious, and unforgiving Mekong/Nam Kading Delta. We were at the mercy of whatever was floating downstream. There was no chance to think. Even if there was, none of my fragile human strategies at the time would have worked, especially in the middle of a fast-churning whirlpool in the darkest of nights. I didn't know how many more minutes I could survive. One thing my niece and I did, though, was to keep each other from becoming disoriented in the whirlpool. We did have the Snake Mountain as a signpost on the Laos side and flatlands and the street lights on the Thai front. So when we saw the rising mountains on the clear sky ahead, we reminded each other not to push forward (because that was the Laotian side), and we attempted to push forward when we saw the flatlands and the street lights ahead.

I didn't know at that time that there was a God in heaven, and that this God would care so much about a sinful human creature like me and would reach out His hands to save me from such a horrific and helpless situation. So I called to my late father. I called out to heaven. I called and begged for whoever would hear and be willing to come to our rescue. At first, I had my clothes on, but after a long night floating in the water, all of my clothes came off of my body. I became totally bare. My niece and I were totally helpless and hopeless. We were as good as dead. Except that we were still breathing – but in the middle of this vast Mekong River in the middle of that September night.

THEY COULD HAVE THROWN MY NIECE AND ME OVERBOARD...

By four or five o'clock the next morning, there was a crew of Thai soldiers who came in a boat. When they approached and saw us, they reached down and plucked my niece and me from the constant churning water. The first question they asked me was, "So where is your money?" By that time, I was already naked. I said to them, "I don't have any money. As you can see, I have nothing on me here." But I now thank God for them, because they had a choice to make. They could have thrown my niece and me overboard since we didn't have the money they were looking for. We would have drowned and that would have been the last of us. My name and personality would have been no more than a memory in the minds of my family and those who knew me. But these Thai soldiers didn't make that choice.

Instead, they gave me a traditional Thai/Lao towel to wear. I was exhausted. And freezing cold. I was shivering. And vomiting with bloodied vomits, I was. I could not stand up. I felt as good as dead. Except that I was still breathing, and able to communicate. The soldiers took my niece and me ashore to their barracks and built a huge fire to warm us up. They cooked a delicious breakfast for us. But I couldn't eat.

As the sun rose over the plain (I presumed about seven o'clock), the captain of the group gave one of the soldiers some money and said, "Take these kids to the bus stop and pay for the fare. Let these kids go and rejoin their family." That company of Thai soldiers took very good care of my niece and me. They made sure my life was saved and that I would have the opportunity not only to reunite with my family but the chance to live a life free from oppression and pursue the opportunities life has to offer in the free world. To this day, I owe my life and my future, in part, to those "good Samaritans." (A word to the wise. You never know when you will become the "good Samaritan" to a stranger, by the little, seemingly insignificant things you do and yet making a life changing impact.)

My niece and I stepped into the bus — and for the first time in my life I did not know where we were going. I had never seen such a huge object called a "bus" or "vehicle" people use to take them places and transport goods even though I had seen planes including helicopters, C-130, T-28 and F-16 Fighter Jets back in Laos in years past. Looking back, when my niece and I were plucked out of the ever-flowing and churning Nam Kading/Mekong delta, our lives were not only being spared, we were one step closer to life and freedom. That meant that our days on earth were prolonged – at least for now. We were supposed to be on our way to be reunited with family members whom we were separated from less than 24 hours earlier, but which seemed like eternity. And we had no clue as to what had become of the rest of the four hundred plus people and my family.

In Luke 10:30-34, Jesus told a similar story of a man who was on a journey. He was being robbed, beaten and left half dead on the road to Jericho. There was a priest who came by on the way and saw the stranger lying there, but he just passed by on the other side of the road. Then a Levite came by and did the same thing. But a Samaritan man came to the robbery victim and had pity on him and took care of him. The story Jesus told not only happened in biblical time. It happened to me. Those Thai soldiers were instrumental in my rescue from the Mekong River and from death to life. Thus was the first Crossing of the River – from political oppression and persecution to freedom. From Freedom Fighters to Political Refugees.

SHE COULDN'T BELIEVE HER EYES...

Meanwhile, there were some people in the group who went to my family and reported that my widowed sister-in-law, my niece, and I had drowned overnight. When my mother heard of the news, she began to mourn for our deaths. She said to my brother Nyaj Hawj, "Throw me back into the river. Let me die after my son. My reason to leave Laos was to take my son so that he can use his eyes to read, his hands to hold pens, his foot to put on shoes, and his body to put on clothes. Now if he is dead, there is nothing for me to live for. Throw me back into the river."

As the sun rose high above the sky, my niece and I were led off the bus where the rest of the group had congregated – in Beurn Kang, a Thai city on the Mekong shores not too far north of where they had landed during the night. (Beurn Kang was south of the Nong Khai Refugee Camp, one of the major Refugee Camps in Northeast Thailand set up and managed by the United Nations High Commissioners for Refugees and the Joint Volunteer Committee [UNHCR and JVC].)

As my mother was weeping and attempting to make sense of what she believed had happened to one of her sons, daughter-in-law, and granddaughter during the night, my niece and I arrived. My mother was ecstatic! She couldn't believe her eyes. In fact, she was crying. But the tears she now shed were tears of joy! Brother Nyaj Hawj said to her, "Mother, your son is here." She couldn't believe it, and to this day she is still ecstatic when she talks about that event.

The refugee journey began. The local police started

counting and recording people's names, dates of birth and relationships. The process of registration started. First finger printing by the local police. Then finger-printing and other elaborate paperwork by Camp personnel, and eventually more elaborate paperwork and oral interviews by Third World Refugee Resettlement Agencies. Thus life as a refugee. In a foreign land. First, in Thailand. Then the U.S. (or wherever a person or family may choose to resettle or be accepted for resettlement). The moment I was plucked out of the dangerous Mekong River currents into the Thai Patrol boat, I became a refugee in a foreign land.

My people had been oppressed, persecuted and hunted as wild animals for the last several years. Now we were on our way to freedom and liberty. But we were in a foreign land and we had a new label – Refugees. And "freedom" didn't seem so wonderful. We were at the mercies of the Thai populace, Thai police officers, Thai and other foreign governments, who now stepped into our lives. Our futures, our destinies were no longer being determined by us, but by someone else. We had no say, whatsoever. Oftentimes, refugees ended up being victims of abuse by local security personnel. Men were being beaten and left for dead. Women were raped. Yet no one could raise a voice to complain or raise a hand to point at perpetrators so that justice – basic human rights justice – could be weighed, let alone accomplished.

As foreign government agencies set up mobile screening centers in the Camp, they had the right and authority to pick and choose those whom they wanted to resettle in their respective countries. This "screening" process ended up dividing and separating families. For some, a family member might end up in Canada while the rest went to the U.S. For others, half of the family might go to France while the rest ended up in Australia. Still for others, while one family member was accepted for resettlement in the U.S., others may end up in New Zealand, Australia, France, or be "stuck" in Thailand, and "disappearing" into the remote villages in northern Thailand. This was the effect of political upheavals on the family unit, especially for people who place such a high value on family relationships as do the Hmong.

FAMILIES WOULD KNOW
WHERE THEY BELONGED...

After the initial registration processes, our family was transported to Nong Khai Refugee Camp. Here we spent eight months. Life in the Refugee Camp was everything but productive and private. Other than socializing and having "fun" inside the Camp compounds, there was not much else anyone could do. Even though there were classes available, including Thai and English as a Second Language, only a few people had the financial resources or the motivation to take advantage of those productive activities. The rest of the refugees lived only a day at a time. There was no direction. No future. No hope. And no life.

**Nongkhai Refugee Camp, Thailand
From left – Cousin Yaaj Pov (passed away March
2012 in St. Paul, MN), Num Huas, T. Cher**

**Nongkhai Refugee Camp, Thailand
From left – Nuj Sua, Num Huas, Nyaj Hawj, T.
Cher, Vaam Pov Front – Niece Maiv Kawm**

As refugees, we were living in an environment where everywhere and everything was common. I mean common in a way that there was no personal space, and there was no personal privacy. The living quarters were 20, 30, or 50 rooms in one huge complex. Multiple families from different geographical locations who knew nothing about one another were crammed together in one space and used one common bathroom. People even shared common cooking spots.

Any shower that people had would be out in the open. Life in the Refugee Camp may be comparable to Minimum Security Prisons here in the U.S

When people are being pushed into a corner, it is amazing how they are able to structure or organize themselves from small group families to extended family, to clan, then to sections. Even though there were common living areas, the unspoken boundaries were still there. This is the unique thing about human structure. Even though there is no written code, there are still boundaries that you cannot cross and you would not cross.

Families would know where they belonged. They would know there were boundaries in a common room and would know that, "This is my area. We can share this as a common room, but this is my private 'room' and you will not cross this un-walled space that I have." They would also have structure with section group leaders and sections where people would say, "If you live in this section, you belong to this group, and if you live in that section, you belong to that group." Even though there was no clear wall boundary, the structure was still very clear. That minimized the confusion of the common known privacy spaces.

On our way to America...
The land of the unknown...
A jungle of another kind...

After eight months in Nong Khai Refugee Camp and a lengthy interview and screening process, my brothers Nuj Sua, Num Huas, Mom, and me were accepted for asylum in the US (Nuj Sua had already registered with the U.S. Resettlement Office in the Camp a few months prior to our arrival in the Camp). Our resettlement status had been posted and departure date set. We were now leaving, not only Laos, but Thailand and the Refugee Camp – to go to Bangkok, the Capitol City of Thailand, before leaving for America. Yes. We had heard about America. We even saw American personnel during the conflict in Laos. My brother Tsaav was even involved with American Advisors for a time. But going to America? Where was America? The picture I had in my mind was that America was a piece of land hanging in mid air. So we were on our way to America... the land of the unknown. America may be the land of the free, but for refugees like me, at least initially, it was the

T. Cher's Asylum ID photo, 1978

land of the unknown. It was the land of the lost. A jungle of another kind.

To us, Laos was a jungle we could see and touch. During and in the midst of our struggles to survive the constant artilleries of the enemies, we were able to navigate our way around. We knew our way in and around the rugged mountains of Laos. It was a place we knew. We were familiar with it. We were used to roaming the jungles there. But as we crossed the Mekong River and the Pacific Ocean, we came into other jungles. Even though these jungles were unlike the ones we roamed in Laos, they were as real and in many ways much more challenging and problematic. More people became the victims, and eventually the American jungles claimed more casualties than that of the jungles of Laos.

June 24, 1979. Into the bus and off we went. We reached Bangkok safely after an eight hour trip from the Nong Khai Refugee Camp. We spent only a few days there for a final check before leaving for America. On the night of June 27, 1979 the four of us made a long and life-altering journey from Don Mueang International Airport, Bangkok, Thailand, to Washington, DC.

AFTER SHE WAS DONE, THE WHOLE BATHROOM WAS FLOODED...

We arrived on the evening of June 29, 1979, and were welcomed into the home of a Hmong family, Yang Chee, who had resettled in the area a few months or even a year prior to our arrival. Once we arrived at our temporary host's residence, mother decided that she needed bath. She was directed to the bathroom, but no one showed her the use of modern household appliances including indoor plumbing and bathtubs. She was (and all of us newcomers were) left to her own devices. She didn't know that in order to have a good bath she needed to step into and lie down inside of the tub and fill it with water. So, instead of filling the bathtub with water before she immersed herself in water in the tub, she filled the tub with water and used the pitcher to pour water on her body – outside of the tub – onto the floor, causing an embarrassing flood in the bathroom. To this day, she still talks about that, and we laugh about that embarrassing moment in her life as a refugee in a foreign land.

NO ONE SHOWED US HOW TO USE THE ELECTRIC APPLIANCES THAT WERE IN THE HOUSE...

After only a few days in our host's home, we moved into our own apartment and attempted to start our new life in America. People were very generous toward us. They brought canned goods, frozen chickens, and other assorted foods. One problem, though. We couldn't use any of the goods we received. We didn't know how to use any of the electric appliances, nor were we able to operate the gas cooking range and its accompanied ovens. So we "fasted for seven days." Later, I would jokingly recount this and other stories about my journey from refugee to "regular," from helplessness to hopefulness and from darkness to light and from death to life. People say that when you cross from one culture to another you experience culture shock. For my mother, two brothers and me, we experienced technological shock!

This was a life altering experience for Mom, my brothers and me. We were alone and lonely. We had left Brother Nyaj Hawj, who, up to that time was the leader of the family who provided security and hope for the rest of us. He was the one who provided a sense of comfort and encouragement to the rest of us, assuring us that no matter how difficult things may seem to be, in the end, things would turn out for the better. After just a short time in our apartment, not knowing how to live there with "modern conveniences," we actually felt futureless, directionless, and hopeless. Brother Nuj Sua then managed to contact cousin Txhaj Vwg and uncle Paaj Ceeb who had come and resettled in Pittsburgh, PA, a few months earlier. Through my cousin, Brother Nuj Sua was able to convince our sponsors to release us so we could be united with relatives.

I continue this journey as a refugee, even to this point. As a person, and as a people, the Hmong were and are homeless, in Laos and through different points of their journey from China to Laos, Thailand, and here in the U.S. Even now, in my life as an American Citizen, a sense of homelessness is still felt inside of me.

Chapter Three

In mid July, 1979, the four us hopped on a bus and made our way to Pittsburgh, PA. Within a couple of days we were able to reunite with uncle Paaj Ceeb and cousin Txhaj Vwg and other relatives. As we resettled in on Pittsburgh's North Side, life seemed to be worry-free for the moment. At first, we had nothing to do and nowhere to be. Eating, drinking, goofing off at local parks, carp-fishing, and soccer-playing were some of the most common activities on a daily basis. In short, life was directionless, and I couldn't have cared less about anything. I didn't know where I was going, what I was going to do, or who or what I wanted to be. I didn't know whether I was going to grow up. So it didn't matter. But Pittsburgh turned out to be a defining place for me economically, academically, socially and spiritually.

September rolled around, and it was time to go to school. A social worker who was Vietnamese, Euai Hueong or Sister Heuong, who spoke Lao, took me to a middle school and attempted to enroll me in sixth or seventh grade. With my background in Lao school and my mastering of the Lao language, Euai Hueong and I were able to communicate. After talking to the counselor or whoever was in the office, she emerged and said to me, "You are too old for this school. We will have to go to a different one and enroll you there."

We went to Allegheny High School and talked to the school. She said to me, "They said you are too old for ninth grade. They are going to put you in tenth grade." I spoke no English. But because of my age (and there was no specialized ESL programs for speakers of other languages) I had to immerse myself in English, and I mastered it as fast as I could. I ended up mingling with mainstream American kids as a tenth grader. By God's grace, I was able to grasp the English language and completed the requirement for graduation from high school in three years.

A PASTOR AND TWO MISSIONARIES KNOCKED ON OUR DOOR...

In the midst of my directionless and hopelessness, God, in his mercy and grace sent people into my life who made a life altering impact on me. Because my life was adrift , like a lot of other young refugees, I was agenda-less also. We had nothing to do. No plans. No schedules. Anything and everything was done at the spur of the moment.

Then, one Sunday morning in the summer of 1980 an Anglo Pastor, accompanied by two former missionaries to Laos, came knocking on our run-down, crowded second floor apartment on Ohio Street. They introduced themselves in Lao as people who served in Laos for several years, and a pastor who had a church nearby. They invited my brothers and me to church that morning.

We accepted their invitation and went with them only out of courtesy and curiosity, and because we didn't want to "hurt" their feelings. At least that was my feeling at the time. Being in the neighborhood as newcomers, we wanted to "fit in." The last thing any of us wanted to do was to offend our "hosts" in the city. Another reason for us to respond so readily at the time was out of curiosity. To us, and to me personally, we had no clue as to what was going on inside those huge buildings on certain days of the week. And we wanted to find out to settle our curious minds.

T. Cher with "Grandpa" Maurice R. Irvin in front of their "home" Cheng in the foreground and Hnou in the background, Toccoa, GA, spring 1986

So we went. When we got to the church building, we were ushered into a college and career class which was in progress. We sat there for an hour. We didn't know what they were talking about, and we couldn't have cared less about anything. After the Sunday School hour, we were ushered to the sanctuary for worship. Again, we knew nothing and couldn't have cared less. After that, I said to myself, "This will be the last time I enter this building." Life went on.

A few months later, I was goofing around in the park one day next to the church. It was about lunchtime, and the pastor, Maurice Irvin, was walking on his way to lunch (I presumed). By that time he remembered my name. He actually greeted me, and he asked me what I was doing. In broken English, I responded that I was just goofing around. Then after that, they came back and engaged me and my brothers and other refugees in the community. They took us under their wings and taught English to us by using the Bible.

Because I was able to grasp the English language more easily than others in the group, I was given the responsibility to interpret to others who were less proficient. As an "interpreter," I had the opportunity to interact with my Anglo (Caucasian) teachers more frequently than others. Because of my relationship with my "teachers," both in school and in church, my English proficiency increased rapidly, and I became the Youth leader in the small refugee "Christian" community.

By cultivating friendships with us refugees, people of

the Allegheny Center Alliance Church community were able to share the gospel with us. Born and raised in an animist home in the mountains of Laos and being the youngest in my family, I felt a strong sense of responsibility and obligation toward my mother. As a Hmong son, the unspoken expectations of my mother and older siblings was that I would take care of my mom in her old age all the way until her last days on earth. It was not an easy thing for me to leave animism and embrace Christianity.

As people from the church continued their friendship with us refugees, they shared with us that there was a Creator God – bigger than the animistic spirits we worshiped – who loved the whole world[6] including homeless and nation-less refugees like us. I understood this truth that God loved me and sent Jesus to die on the cross of Calvary for my sins and I could be forgiven. In Christianity, there was no need for me to sacrifice any animal as an atonement for my sin. In animism, every family member has to be individually "Ua neeb khu" or atoned for in a ritual with an animal, usually a pig, on an annual basis, in addition to participating in such a ritual with the family as a whole. Christianity, or precisely, the gospel of Jesus Christ, taught that Jesus Christ died for sin once and for all[7].

---

6   Jesus said, "For God so loved the world that He gave His one and only Son, that whoever believes in Him shall not perish but have eternal life" – John 3:16.

7   Unlike the other high priests, he does not need to offer sacrifices day after day, first for his own sins, and then for the sins of the people. He sacrificed for their sins once for all when he offered himself. – Hebrews 7:27

I accepted Jesus Christ into my life as my personal Savior and Lord, and I was baptized in December of 1980.

When I was baptized and came out of the baptismal pool, I remember my pastor, who became my spiritual father, announcing to the congregation, "This young man will become a great leader in the church someday." I didn't know whether what he was saying meant anything, and I still don't know if it means anything today, but that started my spiritual journey.

I am reminded of what the Apostle Paul said of himself, as recorded in Scripture, that even before he was born, the Lord God in his great mercy and grace appointed him while he was in his mother's womb for the surpassing greatness of His gospel through Christ. I believe this is true of me, as well. But I am reminded by Scripture that "...by grace I was saved through faith – and this not of myself – it is the gift of God – not by works that no one should boast. For (I was and am) God's workmanship, created in Christ Jesus for good works that (I) should walk in them" – Eph. 2:8-10.

When I became a Christian, my mother was disappointed, to say the least. To her, my accepting Christ dashed her hope of receiving a proper Hmong traditional funeral and burial. To her, my leaving animism meant I was reneging on my responsibility as her youngest son to not only take care of her during her old age, but it also meant I was abandoning her as a mother. She said at the time that all of her love for me and efforts to raise me up to that point were wasted. She actually wanted to be deported back to Thailand to be with my left-behind-brother so that she would receive a proper Hmong traditional funeral and burial.

Against her wish and the wishes of other extended family members, my brothers also decided to follow Christ. We started to pray for my mother that the Lord God would open her heart to understand His love for her. After five years of prayer, she came to see the truth of the gospel and accepted Christ into her life. It was May of 1985 and my mother was with my brothers in the Twin Cities while my family and I were in Toccoa Falls College. One night I received a phone call from Mother. The first question she asked me was, "How can I be baptized?" I asked her why she would ask such a question. She went on to explain: "I have been thinking about you and your brothers lately, and how much I miss you even here on earth. All my life, I have been holding onto your dad's deathbed promise that he would come back for me. But I have been told that the Bible says that Jesus, when He died on the cross, went to hell and preached to the spirits of the dead (referenced I Peter 3:18-19). What if your dad already went to heaven? I don't want to be separated from any of you. I want to follow Jesus, so when I die I can know for sure that I will be with you all in heaven and with Jesus." With that fear and desire, she decided to leave her shamanistic spirits, and to follow Christ and live for him.

I WANTED TO MAKE A NAME FOR MYSELF...

You may recall that back in the days when my home was still in Laos, I wanted to be a Fighter Pilot when I grew up. I wanted to be as famous as Mr. Ly Lue, the only aced Hmong Pilot in my mind thus far. And I wanted to be like him. In short, I wanted to protect my country, but I wanted to do it in such a way that I would make a name for myself.

Now I was no longer in Laos. There was no country to protect. No way to fly a fighter jet. But I still wanted to make a name for my family and myself. So I set my mind on becoming a lawyer. Given the personality type that I have, I could have become a darn good defense lawyer, for that matter! I wanted to be the first Hmong to go to Law School and become the first Hmong Lawyer in America. One of the reasons for such selfish ambition at the time was a strong reaction against others in their attempts to put down my family. You see, my father and his brothers were being called, "Noob Npla Kawm" all their lives.

Let me explain: You may recall that my grandfather Npla Kawm became very poor as a result of the killing of the two chefs during his marriage reception. Consequently, my grandfather and his children became very poor. There is a saying in Hmong that goes like this: "Pluag tsis pluag los pluag cuag taumkib le[8]." Recall that my father was so broke that he was unable to pay for his first wife's dowry nor that of his second wife's, my mother. My mother had to work the poppy fields for at least a couple of seasons to earn enough

---

8   This is a description of the status of an impoverished person/family using a fried soybean. The idea is that as dry and crisp as a fried soybean, so is a person who lives in poverty. My father was very poor before and during his first marriage, and the death of his first wife only worsened his poverty and lowered his status in the community and with the extended family and relatives.

cash to pay for my step-mother's bride price and that of her own. Because of this, my grandfather and his children were looked down upon as unfortunate, undependable, unhelpful, and worth very little when it came to offering any useful advice to relatives and others. My father and his brothers were looked down upon as poor and underprivileged. They were the down and out who were so destitute that they were the laughing stock in the community. I took that to heart, and I wanted to prove to people that I, too, could represent my family. So I planned to succeed.

Thank God, though I struggled, I managed to graduate from Allegheny High School in Pittsburgh in 1982, in three relatively short years.

CHAPTER FOUR

I met my wife and life partner in Pittsburgh, and we got married during my high school senior year. Mai Yia has been my supporter and life partner for more than thirty years. She and her family came to America in 1980 through the sponsorship of her maternal uncle and aunts who resettled in Pittsburgh a few years earlier. Because the Hmong refugee community was a small enclave at the time, we congregated together out of the need for social and emotional support. Even though I knew Mai Yia didn't necessarily like me, I had set my eyes on her and even told a friend that this young woman would be my future wife.

Mai Yia grew up as the second or third child of my in-laws. My father-in-law, Paj Npliam Yaj, disappeared in 1978 on his way from Laos to Thailand, leaving his family behind in Laos. Unbeknownst to Mai Yia, her mother, and her siblings, her father had been captured and killed by enemies shortly after he left his family in the field. They assumed that their father had made it to Thailand safely, and that one day he would be coming back to take them back to Thailand – a place of freedom and liberty, hope and future.

Mai Yia related to me her story of survival, which she termed, "Dead-leftover." She and one of her sisters, Mai Nhia, survived a deadly mushroom poison ordeal while on the trail with her family and other refugees in an attempt to leave Laos. As Mai Yia's family (with numerous other people) attempted to flee Laos, the refugees trekked through rugged mountains and thick jungles for days and days. The food they brought along had become scarcer as their journey of days became weeks. Because of the scarcity of food, people foraged whatever they could find – roots, fruits, leaves, and whatever else they could find that was edible. Mai Yia's family came upon a sizable single mushroom – possibly 8"-12" in diameter and foraged it. At breakfast time, the family managed to roast the mushroom on hot coals, hoping for a decent meal. And they all ate the mushroom for breakfast.

After mealtime, they broke camp and were on the move again. As they started moving, Mai Yia and her sister became disoriented and stumbled. They fell to the ground. The sisters became unconscious while the rest of their family watched. They were as good as dead. To the traveling refugees, the girls were dead. But not to their father, Paj Npliam. Because of the fear of encountering enemy forces on the way, the group leaders began to talk about burying the two young girls and moving on. As Mai Yia's father was being urged to "get done with burying your dead kids and move on," he refused the pressures of the group. "You move on ahead," he replied. "As for me, I would be as good as dead if my girls are not with me." He decided to part ways with the group and surrender himself and his family to the Communist government troops to save his two daughters.

He made his way to a Lao Theurng (Phubthawj) village not too far from where his daughters ate the poisonous mushroom. To his surprise, some of the villagers were his old business acquaintances during peace time several years back. The villagers and his old business associates came to his family's rescue." After their surrender to the Communist government, they were transported back to Ban Sohn and Nasou. Because Paj Npliam was longing for life and liberty, freedom and prosperity for his children, his heart was never at rest.

He was constantly searching for ways to lead his family out of the oppression in Laos under the new regime. Paj Npliam left his family behind and risked his life to find freedom in Thailand. His life was terminated, however, by the local Hmong authorities who thought they could please the Communist government by arresting and executing anyone they believed had planned to escape Communist rules. His dream for freedom from fear was crushed as he was killed.

**Mai Yia's parents Paj Npliam Yaj with her
older sister Mos Lis in early sixties**

Eventually Mai Yia, her mother, and siblings made their
way across the Mekong River and into the Nongkhai

Refugee Camp in 1979. After spending a few months in the Nongkhai Refugee Camp they were transferred to the Ban Vinai Refugee Camp. It was there in Vinai that they were accepted for resettlement in the U.S. and settled in Pittsburgh on June 20, 1980.

After they arrived in Pittsburgh, her family was introduced to the same church I was going to. She became the song leader, I was the leader of the Youth group, and she was sort of my right-hand person. Through that interaction, we came to know each other better. I found out that she actually liked me, and I actually liked her. As a result, we clicked. We fell in love, got married, and she has been my life partner for over 30 years.

My family put a lot of hope in me. In my leadership position at the church, I was now, in the eyes of my family, a rising star in a small way. So when I announced to them I was getting married, they were furious and disappointed. They were in a way saying to me that their hope in me was dashed. There was a political position they were hoping for me to get, but once I got married, that hope vanished, and so they were very angry. Maybe in a very strong reaction to that, I said to myself, "I am going to prove to my family that despite their disappointment in me, one day I will prove them wrong and that marriage did not and will not deter me from accomplishing my educational goal." I have not been there yet. I still have a long way to go. But I have come very far and become a sort of useful vessel for my family.

T. Cher and Mai Yia with Pa Houa and Mom, in the backyard of the apartment on James Street, Just across from General Hospital on the Northside of Pittsburgh, PA, spring 1983

"Grandpa" Maurice R. Irvin with Mai Yia, the kids, and brother Num Huas, Toccoa, GA, spring 1986

CHAPTER FIVE

One day, my pastor, Maurice Irvin, asked me, "Would you be interested in being a pastor?" I said to him, "So what's a pastor do?" He said very simply, "A pastor is doing what I am doing now," pointing to his Bible and explained his devotion to serve his congregation through preaching, teaching, and pastoral caring for his congregation. I knew nothing about theology and Christian education, but I responded affirmatively to him, "Whatever you ask me to do, I will do."

In the meantime, I continued my desire and dream of becoming a lawyer to make a name for myself. I attended a community college for a year in hopes of prepping myself for law school. In the summer of 1983, however, my pastor helped me apply for admission to Bible School. I was accepted at Toccoa Falls College, Toccoa Falls, GA.

Toccoa Falls, the signature and namesake of Toccoa Falls College, T. Cher's alma mater. It is situated in foothills of the Smoky Mountains in Northeast Georgia

On June 10, 1983, my wife and I with our ten-month-old daughter Pa Houa, packed up a couple of pillows that we had and $250.00 in our pocket, and a little lunchbox that my mother and mother-in-law packed for us, we hopped into my pastor's car and off we went. You might say, "To Bible College? Really?" But that's what we did. After a long day's car ride, Pastor and Mrs. Irvin dropped us off in Louisville, Kentucky, while they visited her mother in nearby Lexington. They came back after a week, put us back in their car, and drove us to northeast Georgia where we entered a small town called Toccoa. Population, 12,000. I enrolled in Toccoa Falls College, founded in 1907 by the late Dr. R.A. Forest and his wife as an institution to prepare God's people to fulfill their calling.[9] After four years, I graduated from college with a Bible theology degree in 1987.

WE DIDN'T HAVE ANYTHING EXCEPT EACH OTHER AND GOD...

When my pastor/spiritual father took us to Georgia, he said jokingly as we were on the road, "I am going to take you to a city, a very big city, and you will enjoy it." I believed him. But when we got there, Toccoa was much different than I pictured in my mind. The town was... small. There was only one traffic light in the main district, and the population at the time was 12,000. It was very lonely at first. We arrived on campus in the summer and the campus was essentially empty. Only a few faculty and administrative staff and their families were left on campus.

---

9   Toccoa Falls College's website: www.tfc.edu/history.

When we arrived, we didn't have a place to stay, let alone any furnishings, appliances, and/or any related wares to start our college life. Transportation was a challenge. We didn't have a car. We didn't have money. And there were just the three of us. We knew no one. And no one knew that we were coming – to College. We didn't have anything except each other and God. It was a very, very, lonely journey. But this was when we learned to depend on God. For the need of the moment. Not tomorrow, or the day after, but for today. For now.

Before he left for home in Pittsburgh, Maurice, my pastor/spiritual father (who was a good friend of the college president, Dr. Paul Alford), said to the president, "Please take good care of my son and his family, will you?" With that, the president and the vice president of academic affairs, Dr. John McCarthy, worked very hard with Mr. Fred Hanson, the Vice President for Business Affairs and other Campus staff to secure a livable place for my family. After a couple of weeks, a manufactured home was secured, delivered, and set up at the Mobile Home Park nearby the College Campus. To furnish our "new home," the Married Student Association threw us a home furnishings shower. People brought in blankets, bedding, sheets, pots and pans, and other items. Some even donated money, giving us a good start in our transition from refugees to students.

**T. Cher and other students roasting pigs at an
event sponsored by the International Students
Association of which T. Cher was president, Toccoa
Falls College, Toccoa Falls, GA, April 1987**

By God's grace and through Christian love, strangers
showered my family and me more than we had ever had
before this period in our refugee life. Strangers were eager to
lend a hand, from chauffeuring Mai Yia to the grocery store
to get a box of diapers and milk for the kids, to dropping me
off at the local Burger King restaurant, where I found a job
flipping burgers, and picking me up after work. Strangers
became close friends and classmates all throughout my
college years. God had graciously given us three children
in my four years of college education – Cheng, Hnou, and
Hli, were born to us between 1983 and 1987.

If I had to do it over again, I would, because those were the
good old days: no money, but no bills to pay. No worries.

Life was simple. And God has been so good to us. We had so much peace and so much joy without any major concerns in those four years.

I SPENT TWO DAYS IN THE HOSPITAL, AND I THOUGHT I WAS GOING TO DIE...

It was the last day of my college career. It was my final class. I remember sitting in my professor's office taking my Old Testament final exam. As I started to write, I felt something on my nose. I thought it was a runny nose, and I wiped it off without even looking at it. Then I continued writing the exam for thirty seconds. Another drop. Wiped it off and looked at it. Blood. I had a bloody nose. I ended up in the hospital two hours later. I spent two days in the hospital, and I thought I was going to die.

The doctors didn't know the cause. I still remember to this day what the doctors said to me, "Nosebleed is pretty common, just like women with their monthly menstrual period. Whenever it wants to bleed, it just bleeds."

I could not do anything but put my faith and hope in God and trust in the trained hands of the medical team to treat the now seemingly unstoppable nosebleed. God was gracious to me. Before long, the doctors were able to stop the bleeding, which allowed me to rest.

I had a young family. Four children and a wife. I was ready to walk the aisle with my cap and gown on to receive my bachelor's degree in Bible theology, which I had been working so hard for the past four years. And now I was lying in a hospital bed with my mouth, nose, and face all covered up with gauze. I thought I was going to die, and I didn't know what my wife and kids were going to do.

Then I prayed for God to heal me. My college family prayed for me, my classmates, professors, and the administrators that knew me all prayed for me. Because of that, I recovered. I was able to walk the aisle and receive my diploma. That was another benchmark in my life as I journey Crossing the River. This time it was crossing the Spiritual and Academic River. I was then standing on the shores of a River called Academic Achievement. That day when I walked the aisle to receive my diploma from the hands of College President Dr. Paul Alford, with my classmates and my family in the audience, I knew that as God had superintended my crossing the Mekong River eight years earlier, He was then superintending my graduation from College as well.

T. Cher shaking Dr. Paul Alford's hand while receiving his Bachelor's degree during commencement, Toccoa Falls College, May 6, 1987

After four years in college, with a college degree and four children and a family, God had been faithful in providing all of my financial needs. My college tuition was paid for, my living expenses were paid for, and all of the hospital bills from when we had three children were paid for. We were grateful. Those were the provisions that God gave to us.

Chapter Six

They called me and invited me to come...

After I graduated from Bible College, my wife and I were called to pastor at the Lao/Hmong Alliance Church in Detroit, MI. We came to Detroit in June of 1987, and we pastored that Hmong church for three years.

It took my family and me three months to familiarize ourselves with Detroit and its environment, and to navigate our way around without getting lost. The city's geographic make up was vast and flat. You would not know the directions from east to west, or north to south, except for the rising and setting of the sun. Besides the flat landscape of the city, Detroit, in its former glory, was the Automobile Capital of the world, including the Ford Automobile company founded by its namesake Henry Ford. The company was incorporated in 1902 and headquartered in Dearborn, MI, a suburb of Detroit proper.[10]

When my family and I arrived on the scene in 1987, however, we found a totally different city. For the most part, the city's North side had started to deteriorate years earlier as the auto industry and related businesses were either downsized or moved out completely, even long after the Great Depression. According to Wikipedia, Ford was one of only a few auto manufacturing companies that survived the Depression, and remains the third auto manufacturing company in the world today.

The city was so depressed that when we moved into Detroit, the median price for a three bedroom house in our neighborhood was $15,000. $15,000.00 for a house? That's right. It was cheaper than a new Ford! Even so, it took us three months to find a home for our family, as we began our pastoral work.

We ended up spending our first three months of pastoral work living with the head elder of the congregation, Txawj Pov Tsaab and his family. We are grateful for his hospitality in allowing my family to "squeeze" in with his growing family, as they provided a roof over our heads and shared other resources with us.

---

10   Wikipedia History of Ford Motor Company as recorded on http://en.wikipedia.org/wiki/History_of_Ford_Motor_Company.

**T. Cher with the youth group of Warren Hmong Alliance
Church (formerly Lao/Hmong Alliance) in Michigan
at a retreat center in northern Michigan, 1993**

Meantime, the rest of our family's belongings (the books
I acquired during my College years, my wife's traditional
Hmong clothing given to her as gifts from relatives when
we first married five years prior, and other items we had
acquired over the last few years), were put into Txawj
Pov's brother-in-law, Nyiaj Huas Vaj's basement a couple
of blocks away. Because of the mostly flat landscape
of the area, a heavy rain poured down for a couple of
hours and flooded his basement. Unbeknownst to us,
but the little we had and stored in the basement were
soaked, and most of the items were destroyed. (Little did
we know that some 20 years later, one of Nyiaj Huas's
daughters would become my daughter-in-law. I had the
privilege of officiating my son Cheng and daughter-in-law
Aong Vang, Nyiaj Huas's daughter's wedding in the now

Warren Hmong Alliance Church in Warren, MI, just outside of Detroit proper.)

After three months with the Txawj Pov Tsaab family, in September we finally made an offer for a house not too far away. We bought the house for a mere $22,000.00. And we thought that was expensive! The Lord God provided the resources for us, though, to acquire that house, and we called it home during our three years of ministry in Detroit. We are grateful for families like Uncle and Aunt Neej Thoob Yaj who readily lent us the needed financial resources to secure the house.

What did I learn from this short experience in Detroit? Let me share a couple. Remember what I said about the vastness of the geographical landscape of Detroit? Fresh out of College with a theological education under my belt, I was ready to forge my way into people's lives with the zeal and zest in my heart and cram down their throats the theological knowledge I had just acquired. I wanted to shake people up, and I demanded that they change… or else… God would flash his judgment on them. I learned very quickly that that's not the way to approach people. I was not the boss. I was (and all of the Hmong pastors were) seen as mere employees. The elders control what's going on in the church and the church life for that matter.

I also learned very fast that I may have the education, but people in the church knew the Lord way better. I was told to my face on at least a couple of occasions, "Pastor, you may have the education but remember, we have known Jesus for over 30 years and have more experience than you.

OK?" How do you respond to such insulting comments, especially from someone you thought were your friends? I thank God that he gave me a calm response at the time. So I said, "You're right. I may have the education and the degree, but you have the experience and wisdom. I am here not to lead you but to learn from you. I need your leadership and guidance so we together can lead the congregation to honor God and reach out to others."

An older Anglo pastor once told me, "Cher, respect has to be earned." I didn't know what he meant at the time. But as I got older, I began to understand that in order for people to respect me, I needed to demonstrate to them that I deserved their respect. That's human nature and behavior. I took that admonishment to heart and let it grow. Overtime, I have begun to see the fruit of that subtle but profound comment in my life and in the life of others.

An old, "uneducated" pastor often said to me whenever he saw me or had the occasion to be with me, "Txhaj Cawv ov, mej cov hluas mas has le yug ua. Ua le yug has xwb txhale zoo." Translation? "Txhaj Cawv, you young people preach what you practice. Practice what you preach." During my College days, one of my professors said during one of the classroom sessions, "People do not care how much you know until they know how much you care." This statement made a lasting impact on my ministry.

In summary, the three main things I learned during my short ministry tenure in Detroit were, first, humility. Humility is power. It takes power to humble oneself in the midst of potentially explosive situations. The Bible says, "The fear of the Lord teaches a man wisdom and humility comes before honor." – Prov. 15:33. I have learned, and continue to learn, that honor can only be given to whom honor is due. Humility comes before honor. Another Scripture says, "Before his downfall a man's heart is proud, but humility comes before honor" – Prov. 18:12.

Secondly, respect has to be earned. Before people respect you, you have to prove yourself to be respected. The Apostle Paul exhorts young Timothy with similar words when he said, "Don't let anyone look down on you because you are young, but set an example for the believers in speech, in life, in love, in faith and in purity" – I Tim. 4:12. In short, don't do anything just for a show. Do things to show the way you, yourself, are traveling.

Thirdly, leadership. Leadership is a broad term and countless books have been written about it. Conferences on leadership have become some of the most attractive events in our day. People talk about leadership from one-on-one meetings between two people, to thousands attending workshops, to popular radio and TV shows – all about leadership. But it comes down to doing what you do with humility and to the best of your ability. And never stop learning to lead and to follow. What I've learned is that a leader ultimately helps those who are in need of leadership to accomplish what they need to get done in such a way that, in the end, the people say, "We did it ourselves."

In 1990, we learned of an opportunity in the Twin Cities to plant a church. This Hmong church group was part of an Anglo church—Calvary Baptist Church in Roseville, Minnesota. They had been led by an Anglo pastor-turned-missionary who was due to be leaving for the mission field in Asia. This Hmong group was looking for a Hmong pastor to come and lead them to the next level of their spiritual journey. They invited me to come.

As a result of this invitation, we moved to St. Paul in June of 1990 to plant this Hmong church. It was called Hmong Faith Baptist Church and was affiliated with the Baptist General Conference. After two years into this church planting, I received a generous fellowship from the Bush Foundation which was established by the late Archibald Granville Bush, chairman of the executive committee of the 3M Company and his wife Edyth Bassler Bush's Leadership Fellows Program.[11] This fellowship afforded me the opportunity to go back to seminary. I resigned from Hmong Faith Baptist Church as their senior pastor and started full time at Bethel Seminary in St. Paul.

MY HEART BEGAN TO ACHE...

After two years of seminary education, I completed my program (receiving a Master of Arts degree in Theological Studies) and came back to pastoring another church, the Twin Cities Hmong Alliance Church. While pastoring this church, the Hmong families at the time had been in a lot of challenges. Children were joining gangs at a very young age. Couples were deserting each other for strangers. In essence, Hmong families were disintegrating.

---

11   Additional information can be found on the Bush Foundation's website at www.bushfoundation.org/history.

As I read the newspaper and watched the news reports on television, my heart began to ache about the disintegration of Hmong families as they continue their journey into America in search of the American Dream. God seemed to speak to my heart to do something about these Hmong issues. As I read the Bible, the Spirit of God began to stir my heart through the story of Esther. The Bible says Esther was an orphan girl who was raised by her uncle Mordecai during the reign of Xerxes of Persia. Through a series of events, Esther came to the palace of Xerxes and replaced Vashti, the king's divorced wife, and became queen in her place.

Meantime, Haman, an official of King Xerxes plotted to exterminate Esther's people, the Jews, because of his hatred toward Mordecai and his insubordinate behavior and actions. Mordecai found out about the plot and reported to Esther about the impending disasters that would befall the Jews if she did not do anything about it. Mordecai's words to Esther were: 'Do not think that because you are in the king's house you alone of all the Jews will escape. For if you remain silent at this time, relief and deliverance for the Jews will arise from another place, but you and your father's family will perish. And who knows but that you have come to royal position for such a time as this?' – Esther 4:13-14 - NIV.

As the Spirit tugged at my heart, leading me to compare myself to Esther, I rationalized, "But I am not in the king's palace like Esther was, and I don't have the influence or the ability to influence people in authority like that of Esther." Then the words of Jesus as recorded in Matthew 19:26 came to me, "With man this is impossible but with God, all things are possible." And God's Word in another place challenged me when I read, "Not by mightn or by power, but by My Spirit, says the Lord Almighty" – Zechariah 4:6.

You see, I didn't go to school to learn about non-profit organizations and raising funds to support my family and myself so I can do the work of the ministry. Rather, I studied Bible and theology to preach and lead people to Christ. Starting a non-profit organization and writing proposals? Asking people for money? No. In fact, I didn't know that people would actually give their hard earned money away for others in order to make a difference in the lives of those who are less fortunate.

Then I wrote my burden onto a piece of paper and sent it off to a Christian businessman I knew of, telling him about the burden the Lord God had put in my heart for the Hmong families, telling him what I would like to see and what I would like to do. My letter went out for three months. I never expected anything back from him or anyone else for two reasons: First, I had not met him personally. So based on our relationship status at the time, I doubted he would entrust me with his financial resources. Secondly, I did not know whether he had any money to give away so freely without checking the qualifications of people who requested gifts from him… like me.

I FOUND A TEN THOUSAND-DOLLAR CHECK…

One day I went out to the mailbox and I found a letter from this Christian businessman. In this letter was a $10,000 check. In the accompanying letter, this man wrote, "Cher,

I give you this gift to do with the Hmong families in a way in which God calls you." I didn't know what to do with that check,. I actually put it in my briefcase and carried it for the next three months. Anytime I opened my briefcase, the check was staring at me, reminding me, and actually haunting me, for that entire period of time.

Then eventually, in December of 1995, a small organization called Family & Youth Advancement Services, Inc. came into being. The ministry was registered with the State as a non-profit ministry and a 501(c)(3) status from the IRS was granted soon after. Even though Family & Youth Advancement Services, Inc. was established and ready to serve, I was not willing nor ready to step out to serve the needs of the Hmong community. My rationale at the time was that before I committed to full-time service in the newly formed and fragile ministry, sufficient funding had to be in place.

Family & Youth Advancement Services, Inc. logo, St. Paul, MN, 1995-2005

another church in East St. Paul. This time it would be a cross cultural church. Scripture is pregnant with stories of people who were called by the Lord God into unknown places to accomplish His work of redemption and transformation of others. God called Abram out of the Chaldeans to go and be a blessing to the nations (Gen. 12:1-5); Moses was called to return to Egypt to lead God's people out of the land of slavery and bondage and into the land flowing with milk and honey; Joshua was called to conquer the land of Canaan; the Judges were called to deliver God's people from bondage and oppression into freedom and liberty; Samuel was called to bring God's people back to Himself; Saul and David were called to shepherd God's people; the prophets were called to call God's people, who had gone astray, back to himself; Jesus himself called disciples to follow Him, and He gave them the charge to go and preach the gospel to all nations. Throughout the history of the Christian Church, Christ-followers also have been called to go to unknown places and preach the gospel to strange tongues and languages.

So our call to a cross cultural church planting was not peculiar, nor was it strange. We were just following what we believed the mandate the Lord God has laid in our hearts as a family. What was unusual, however, was that my wife and I were former refugees from war-torn Laos and now were being considered for church planting work – cross-culturally – with the launch team being mostly Caucasians.

"If you had the chance to do church again, what would you like to see?" was the question posed to me when I met with one of the future church planting team members. Cheryl

Bostrom and I were introduced to one another through a pastor in the neighborhood, and we sat down to get better acquainted. As the conversation progressed, it revolved around ministry and ministry calling. When Cheryl posed that original question, I paused for a minute and responded: "If I had the opportunity to do church again, I would like to see a church full of people from all ethnic backgrounds worshipping God in one location at the same time."

That was the initial conversation Cheryl and I had. Time passed. The passion was burning bright in Cheryl's and her husband, Matt Bostrom's hearts. The Bostroms and others started to "court" me about the idea of a multi-cultural church on the Upper Eastside of St. Paul. As my wife and I were being wooed, I told the Bostroms and others that we would be praying for and about whether the Lord was calling us as a family to such a church planting work.

As I was praying, the Lord seemed to whisper to my heart: "Cher, I want you to consider this: Over half a century ago, white missionaries left their families and homes to come to the jungles of Laos to share the gospel with your people. Now it's your turn to minister to them here in the Upper Eastside of St. Paul." I was surprised to hear this in my heart, so I came home to share with my wife what I had just "heard." She agreed that maybe this was what the Lord God was calling our family to – to be a part of a multi-cultural church plant.

We met with the North Central District of the Evangelical Free Church of America's Church Planters assessment team, and after a long day of conversation and evaluation, the team discerned that the Lord indeed had called us to be a part of this church planting team on the Upper Eastside. We accepted the call and became a part of the team.

As my family and I embarked on this cross cultural church planting journey, we learned at least two very important lessons about cross cultural awareness and acceptance. When it comes to cultural awareness, I wanted to believe, in my 30-plus years of living in and working with mainstream America that I had become pretty aware of the majority's cultural values and practices, and, therefore, I should be able to minister to my congregants' needs (most of whom are of the majority culture). However, I initially found myself feeling very awkward when it came to ministering to my congregation's needs.

By the same token, many of those in the congregation whose backgrounds are of the majority culture initially found it awkward to fellowship with those of minority cultures. Even though unconsciously, those of the majority culture expect those of us in the minority cultures to communicate with and to them in proper English (since we live here now), only to find out that at times, our English skills are much more limited than expected.

I have also come to realize how I prefer to be with "birds of the same feather," even though there is a biblical principle of inclusivity under the cross of Christ. It took four years from that first meeting with Cheryl until the Cross Cultural Church was established. I still pastor there, and I am still growing.

When the Lord God called Abram out of Ur of the Chaldeans he blessed him and said to him that he would make him a father to many nations. My wife and I were reminiscing about our involvement with CrossCultural church planting recently. We were amused and humbled to realize that the Lord God is so gracious in giving us this privilege of becoming "parents of many nations" both spiritually and biologically.

Things begin to change...

Family & Youth Advancement Services, Inc. (FYASI) served as an independent ministry from 1997 through 2005. As a small faith-based organization, we were doing just fine until the event of the terrorist attacks in New York City, Pennsylvania, and Washington, D.C., on September 11, 2001.

The events of 9/11 affected a lot of organizations. In fact, I would say it affected everyone, not just here in Minnesota or in the Twin Cities or in America, but globally. A lot of smaller organizations actually closed their doors due to the dwindling of financial support. Family & Youth Advancement Services was no exception.

That event negatively impacted the funding of my ministry, and brought stress on me. And then came my brother Nuj Sua's death (described earlier), and I became very, very depressed. I began to gain a lot more weight than my body could handle. My physical health was at stake.

I was so depressed that I felt there was no one on this planet except me. I felt so alone and so lonely. I was praying to God and said, "God, why is this happening to me? My ministry is struggling to survive and now my brother's illness is getting worse. I feel like no one else on this earth cares about me or who I am or what I am going through." Through this "valley of the shadow of death,"[12] the Lord God was faithful to me. In the midst of this imminent dissolution of the ministry of FYASI, and death of my brother who was one of my best friends, the Lord God granted a peace that the Apostle Paul exhorts believers to claim in Philippians 4:7, saying, "And the peace of God, which transcends all understanding, will guard your hearts and your minds in Christ Jesus."

As the Board of Directors of FYASI began a discussion regarding the direction of the ministry and its potential impacts, not only on the staff and their families but also those we served and the community, I made a conscious decision not to throw in the towel. I informed the board that I would not change anything and would continue to do what God had called me to do, until He informed me otherwise. I believed this organization/ ministry was not mine—it was God's. If the Lord God wanted the organization to close the door and fold, that was His prerogative. Not mine. What I needed to do was to remain obedient to the call He had placed in my life.

One of the FYASI's board members, whose husband served on the Union Gospel Mission's board of directors at the

---

12   King David said of the Lord God that because He was his Shepherd, he was not in want, even when he walked through the valley of the shadow of death. He said God's rod and staff would guide and protect him, and he would dwell in the house of the Lord God all the days of his life – Ps. 23.

time, suggested a conversation with the Mission regarding potential partnership moving forward in serving the needs of the Hmong community in St. Paul. We made an appointment with the Mission's Executive Director at the time, Ken Cooper.

I went into his office and shared about my journey from Laos to the U.S. and from lostness to being found in Christ, and God's call in my life to serve Him in this capacity and my vision and passion. He said to me, "The Mission has been talking about serving the Hmong community and meeting their needs, but we do not have the inside expertise, and/or skills to meet their needs. We do have the resources, and we would love to talk about that further." Mr. Cooper assured me that I would have an opportunity to share my vision and passion with the Mission's Board at their next meeting. He then included me in their next meeting agenda where I was invited to share the needs of the organizations of Family & Youth Advancements Services, Inc. After hearing my personal journey and the call of God in my life, the Mission's board voted unanimously to make Family &Youth Advancement Services, Inc., part of the Mission. Because of that, we merged with the Mission in February of 2005, becoming Asian Ministries of the Union Gospel Mission Twin Cities.

"YOU ARE THAT TREE..."

One day in 2003, when I was driving on my way to cross the Lafayette/U.S. highway 52 Bridge to pick up my wife from work and contemplating the loneliness I was experiencing, and how hopeless and bleak my future seemed, I all of a sudden heard a voice in my head, and a picture was painted in my mind. I saw a well-trodden trail going up a hill. It was so trodden that it was very, very dirty and trenched.

On the side of the trail was a tree, and the trunk was marked with both old and fresh cuts. Half of the roots were exposed because of the frequent pounding rain drops and the constant treading on the nearby trail by pedestrians. This tree also served as an object for travelers to lean on. The tree's physical location on the hillside provided a convenient object for the heavy-laden travelers to lean on and catch their breath before moving on to their next destination. Despite the disfigured trunk and the exposed roots of the tree to the abuse of nature, the leaves were still very green and lush.

A voice came to my head and said to me, "Cher Moua, you see this tree? Even though the roots have been exposed and the trunk has been marked with cuts and injured, the leaves are still so green and lush. Do you know why?" The voice continued, "I still take care of that tree. I still bring the rain and the sunshine to nurture this tree. Even though the tree has been cut on the trunk and the roots have been exposed, the tree flourishes. It still stands to serve my purpose – as an object for weary and heavy-laden travelers to lean on and to catch their breath before they move on to their next destination. You are that tree. You may feel depressed and lonely, you may feel bruised or injured, but you are that tree. Life is a journey. People will become tired. They will become lonely. They need 'a tree' to lean on. I will use you to encourage those people on their journeys. People with relationship issues, family conflicts, and other personal needs can be encouraged and challenged. They will be strengthened to take their journey to the destination I have prepared for them.

"After they lean on that tree, they regain their strength to move on in their journey. For others when they get to that tree, they see the tree as a target to practice their cutting skills. They will try their machetes and their knives, and they will cut the tree. But remember, I still take care of the tree. I am taking care of you so you can be a tree for people who are heavy-laden to come to and lean on for encouragement and counsel on their journey to their next destination."

Realizing the implications of this "still small voice" in my heart and mind, telling me that the Lord God loved me so much and called me to serve Him and give me a purpose to live – not for me, but for others and for Him, tears of gratitude began to stream down my face. I could not help but praise him for his great mercy and grace on such a depressed servant as me.

That experience took place when I was in the midst of my discouragement, my depression. So was this episode an illusion? Or was it an answer to my depressed cry for assurance and direction? Looking back, I believe it was a message from the Lord God assuring me that I was important to Him. When I was in the lowest of lows, the Lord reached down and whispered to my heart, assuring me of his grace and mercy. The Lord God had given me that assurance, that I was important, not because I was anybody, but because he was and is God. And he had chosen to use such an earthen vessel as me. Now any time that I have any challenges in my life, I go back to that instance in my life and remember that God is still watching over me and he will take care of me even to the very end of my life's journey here on this planet earth.

HMONG *Christian Herald*

Volume 1, No. 1 • February 26, 1999 • FREE

Rev. T. Cawv Muas, Editor

Hmong Christian Herald: Ntawv Xuvxwm Moob Hab? Leejtwg Tseem Yuav Yuav?

by Rev. Txhaj Cawv
Monanoxou, Editor

Hmong Christian Herald: Another Hmong Newspaper? Who Needs It?

by Rev. Txhaj Cawv
Monanoxou, Editor

Famine strikes

More than 15,000 Minnesota tweens will help the world's hungry by going without food Feb. 26-27. Supported by pledges from families and friends, they will join more than 600,000 young people across the U.S. in the "World Vision 30-hour famine," which is now called to raise nearly $8 million for hunger-fighting programs. Many participants will take part in service projects during the "famine." Students in Watertown will serve food at a Minneapolis soup kitchen, while students in Sartell will support a local food bank by "borrowing the food."

101

Ker Cobqhia Menyuam Ntawv Xuvxwm Moob Hab?

continued from page 5

ua nroj ua ntiv ntawd tais yog ib qhov zoo.

6. Moob opbxwm. Muaj qee lub lav tais pub nplawm menyuam tiamsis yog menyuam phem tihau hwv lawm, yus yeej muaj cai xuas rau nplawm me me nplawm. kom menyuam paub hais tias yus rau txim rau rau nws.

Tiamsis tsis txhob ntau rau kom tus pom, tihob tus txhob ntaus kom nws doog. ua koua kua xuhau. Thaum koj nplawm, koj tsis txhob cia li xuas tib tog kom; nws sab kiag xwb, tiamsis nloob tos nplawm me me coj los nplawm. Koj yuav tsum xub qhia nws lub txim rau nws tag koj mam li nplawm. Koj mee ntom nplawm ib tog uo xos. Koj nplawm, koj tsis txhob nplawm ib tog muob mob xwb cia xuas, tiamsis yuav tsum nplawm li 5-10 tog xwb ntawm lub txim koj los mee. Koj ua tus nplawm tihiab kom nws ua rau nuav, rau qhov tsis yog koj nplawm mes xwb tiamsis yog nws nplawm mes thob. Vajtookub yeej qhia kom peb yuav tsum nplawm peb cov menyuam uas tais tsim txiaj [Paljug 13:24; 22:15; 23:13;29:15).

7. Yog koj cob qhia tsis tau lawm, koj yuav tau coj mus rau kom qee pab koj cob qhia. Nug tou tiom tej lub cercvcom, tej chaw pab pejxeem (social ser-vice agencies) saib puas muaj yam tais yuav pab tau koj. Ib qhov tihwjneeb yog thov Vajtswv pab nws. Vajtswv yog tus tsim peb, Vajtswv thiaj yog tus uas yuav hloov tau peb.

Peb mus yuav khoom ces kuag nnsab li phau ntawv cua qhia rau peb coj los dhos yam khoom thiab siv yam khoom ntawd, tiamsis thaum peb muaj ib tug menyuam, tsis muaj ib phau ntawv neeg tus menyuam ntawd los rau peb cov ua niam ua tav kom peb paub pab nws. Tiamsis tsawm yog tsis muaj phau ntawv ntawd los, peb muaj cuab kav kawm ntawm lwm tus. Peb yuav tsum tau mus nug lwm tog uas tsog cob qhia tau luag tej menyuam tais haug cob qhia li cas. Coj koj tsev neeg mus nrog lej yim uoj tej mentyuam nrhog luo nyob ib sab hnub thiab koj ua tib zoo kawm saib luag cob qhia luag cov menyuam li cas.

Kuv xav kom peb tsis txhob yuav tsis tsis kev cwjpwm tas yus tsoo yus xeb, tsis thov hom tas pub yus thiab tais kaim kawm ntawm lwm tus. Tus neeg uas tsis thov lwm tus pab thiab tsis kaim kawm ntawm lwm tug, tus ntawd mus tsamlos no tsis nyob ntawd lawm. Xyaum qee yam li uas hais los saum no nuav rau uj uas koj mos lawm, kuv ntseeg hais tias koj yuav muaj kev kaj siab thiab ua neej nyob zoo siab so.

continued from cover

ntsuiplig ua txiamyog peb yuavtsum xave taug hab ntuab peb lub sab lub ntsws rau Nwg kaav tuagnrho lug ntawm qhov kws peb hloov dhua sab tshiab ntsug.

Log ntawm Family & Youth Advancement Services lub Hmong Christian Herald, peb tejtxoj sab yuav tuv qtom ntxhas cov kws nyeem ntaub xuv nuav taug qhov kws Yexus hau tawg Nwg tugkheej hnoue tej ntawd.

ntsuiplig ua txiamyog peb yuavtsum xave taug hab ntuab peb lub sab lub ntsws rau Nwg kaav tuagnrho lug ntawm qhov kws peb hloov dhua sab tshiab ntsug.

Lub hontpubaj thleh ib ntoom Hmong Christian Herald yog lug cobqha hab tihaalawm Tswv Yexus Txaj Moo zoo rua cov kws tsis tau moog church hab cov tsis tau ntseeg Tswv Yexus. Nyob rua txhua txiab xuv huv Hmong Christian Herald mas peb yuav muaj cov xuvlawvle Vaajtugkoo kws yuav cobqha hab ua cua tuabneeg xaav hab ntuab nwvyim rua tsev tuabneeg Moob txug kev sis tuamxeeb nruabhncab ntawm tsev tuabneeg hab vaj tugkheej, peb yuav muaj nyveum txog tej yaam kwa muaj ntawm tug sijyaam le. Ntawm txhua-txhua neeb peb yuav sim lug txhawb hab tuv ntau tus ua kws muaj kev meetn ntuab xuvneem onav kom puab ug lug txhaug sab Yexus tej kws Nwg hau txug Nwg tugkheej haxtas Nwg yog tug Tswv rua lub ndiajteb hab yog tug Cawmseej ntawm peb xaali

T. Cher on the front page of his newly published newspaper, the Hmong Christian Herald, St. Paul, MN, February 26, 1999 (with generous partnership from then publisher of the Minnesota Christian Chronicles, Michael Beard who currently serves as the Minnesota State Representative from Shakopee, MN)

Mai Yia's brother and sister-in-law Txawj Huas and Lig Yaj when visiting Thailand in 2005

CHAPTER SEVEN

What does it mean to be without a country? It's very lonely. More than that, it's not just a refuge from your homeland. Go back to the early Hmong history. Legend says that the Hmong had a homeland in central China. Some scholars would argue the Hmong Kingdom or the Hmong land was in central China in the Hebei province back in 3000 BC. There were constant conflicts between the Han Chinese and the Hmong. The Hmong kingdom was invaded by the Han Chinese and the Hmong were chased and driven out of their country southward.

Since then, the Hmong, as a people, have never had a homeland of their own. They migrated from China to Burma, Laos, Vietnam, and Thailand, and eventually spread all over the world. Ever since then, the Hmong simply have not had a homeland of their own. Hmong have a saying that is fitting: "Qev luas toj yug yaaj. Qev luas taig rau ntxhai/" Literally, it means "Borrow others' fields to graze your sheep. Borrow others' bowl to hold your broth." It matters very little because wherever the Hmong go, they have no claim of ownership of any kind as far as real estate is concerned. That's the heart of being homeless and stateless.

On a personal level, being a refugee only further complicates the identity of a person. For me, who I am without my identity in Jesus Christ as a Christian, I am a Hmong. But when people ask me where I come from, I would point back to Laos. But was Laos, or Vietnam, or China, or even Thailand the Hmong homeland? A lot of people would say yes. But in actuality, no.

When I was in La Platta, Argentina, in September and October of 1997, the Rev. Ed Sylvoso, President of Harvest Evangelism, encouraged people from 50 different countries at the rally to "come down to the platform and show the country where you are from." I came from the United States of America as an American citizen, yet from Laos as an ex-refugee. But in actuality I had no homeland of my own. As I sat in the balcony of the stadium watching people go forward, the loneliness of being homeless was so acutely painful. I was a human being. Every human is supposed to have a home and a homeland. People are proud of their national symbol, the most important of which is the National Flag. I didn't have one. I didn't represent Laos because I was no longer a Lao citizen. I was an American citizen, but only by Naturalization, not by birth. I was stung by the loneliness of being homeless and country-less.

In the midst of this loneliness, though, I was reminded of the words of Jesus as recorded in John 14:1-3:

Let not your hearts be troubled. Believe in God; believe also in me. In my Father's house are many rooms. If it were not so, would I have told you that I go to prepare a place for you? And if I go and prepare a place for you, I will come again and will take you to myself, that where I am you may be also. And you know the way where I am going.

WE NEVER HAD ANY HOPE OF A NORMAL LIFE AGAIN...

Even though I was born in Laos, in a real sense, Laos was not a Hmong country. So while it is very, very difficult to be a refugee in exile from one's own country or motherland, imagine the difficulty when you are a refugee without a home country. Now, though, I have adopted America as my home, and I consider myself an American, the idea of nationality is still very, very blurred and obscure because I don't have a geographic location to point to and say, "I was born here" and "I call this my country."

When we left our homes, our villages, we did not have any hope in returning home as it was. We never had any hope of a normal life again, so life on the move was normal for us. Life without permanency became a permanent idea for us, at least for me, anyway. In a way, it didn't matter where we settled in the world. No matter where it was, there still was a sense of homelessness, a sense of hopelessness, and a sense of futureless and directionless for the Hmong.

For that sense, I think the word *nomadic* has become or has been a descriptive word for the Hmong life in general. We may live in America, we may live in Thailand, we may live in China, and we may live in Australia. Wherever we may be geographically, the Hmong have no home, and I have no home.

In 1997, my wife and I traveled back to Thailand for the first time in 28 years. We spent three weeks in northern Thailand visiting relatives after we attended a conference hosted by the Hmong Church of Thailand. That trip brought back nostalgic memories. The "good, old days." At least for me, I I felt a sense of loneliness as I saw my birthplace from a distance for the first time in over two decades.

Then, in 2005, my wife and I went back again. This time we had the opportunity to cross over and step into Lao soil for the first time in 33 years. We rode a chartered bus across the "Friendship" bridge from Nongkhai, Thailand, to Vienchan, Laos. Once we arrived at the border checkpoint, I was overwhelmed with a sense of estrangement. A sense that I no longer belonged to this land I was born in some forty-plus years earlier. I was not the only one who sensed the strangeness of being in Laos. The natives looked at me as a foreigner. I was no longer a native of Laos. To them, I was either Japanese, or a Filipino by the way I looked, by my behavior, or even the way I walked. My accent even gave away my foreignness in the land.

CHAPTER EIGHT

As stated earlier, I was born and raised an animist. Animism is a folk religion in the world. I would say now that there are animists all over the world. Animism is a belief system that believes in a supernatural power, whether it's personal or impersonal. The belief is that there's a supernatural, impersonal force or a supernatural personal being that has the ultimate power over human affairs and human obligation. It determines when any events, either good or bad, occur in human life. It determines how this power is affecting the environment and how to take action, either to appease or to correct. I grew up in that environment and my mother was a shaman.

Growing up as a Hmong man, I wanted to be the most effective and helpful person in the Hmong community, closely following expectations of my elders. However, as I grew older, through our experience in Laos and transition to the refugee camp and into America, my beliefs slowly changed, and they changed dramatically as I came in contact with Christianity.

Before Jesus Christ came into my life, my life was hopeless, directionless, and futureless. I didn't know who I was, I didn't know what I was going to do, and I didn't know where I was going. I was homeless, and I was stateless. I related in the last chapter about the burning sensation I had in my heart when I was in Argentina watching people go forward to show their patriotism to their homelands, and I couldn't go forward because Laos was no longer my homeland, but I was not ready to call America my country, either.

At that moment, tears streaming down my face, I thought about how there was no piece of real estate I could put my foot on and say, "This is my home. This is my land." Then all of a sudden, Jesus' assuring words that were recorded in John 14:1–3 came flooding to my mind: "Then Jesus said to his disciples this way, 'Let not your hearts be troubled. Believe in God, believe also in me. In my father's house there are many rooms. If it were not so, would I have told you that I go to prepare a place for you? And if I go and prepare a place for you, I will come again and will take you to myself. Then where I am you may be also.'" I was reminded that even though I was homeless and stateless, someday Jesus is going to come and take me to be with him in heaven. That will be my permanent home forever, and not just for a time.

GOD CALLED ME AND APPOINTED ME...

As far as my spiritual journey and religious convictions, when I came to Pittsburgh, I was homeless, I was directionless, I was futureless, and I couldn't care less. But when Jesus Christ came into my life and I accepted him as my personal Savior and my Lord, I knew that I wasn't able to save myself. I realized that I was a sinful man, and I needed a savior. Jesus is the only savior. He came and he died on the cross and saved me.

So Jesus, in a way, not only saved me spiritually; he actually saved me from the Mekong River. You recall that during my Mekong River experience, I did not know God, and I couldn't care less about him. But I was at the end of my rope, in a sense, when I was going to drown. It was the middle of the darkest night in my life thus far. The river was raging at full flood stage. I called out. I had to. I was drowning. My life was coming to an end. In a terrible way – drowning. I was swimming a circle in a whirlpool between the Mekong River and the Nam Kading. When I called to heaven and the Thai soldiers came and saved me.

How many people were being saved by the Thai soldiers? A lot of people I know and I heard about were being robbed and murdered because they had the money the Thai soldiers wanted. What advantage did the Thai soldiers have to rescue me from the Mekong River, since I didn't have money? What benefit would they have by rescuing an as-good-as-dead refugee boy from who knew where? They didn't have any benefit, yet they rescued me anyway. Looking back, I now know that God had His hand on me, even though I didn't know Him or acknowledge Him. The Bible says that even though I did not know God, He knew me. Before I was born, he appointed me. I know and I believe that God called me and appointed me way before I even realized that there was a God.

MY ROLE IS TO BE THAT TREE...

Since I became a Christian and learned to walk the Christian life and teach Christian principles according to what the Bible and Jesus teach, I have become hopeful. I have purpose, and I have a future. I have come to understand how Jesus wants to use me. I am to be the tree that was been beaten down by the rain and by people who chopped on the tree trunk. There are people who come with heavy loads on their shoulders and their back and lean on the tree. I am to be a pastoral counselor for people who have heavy burdens in their families and marriage relationships. They can come and lean on me and be refreshed, renewed, and regain their strength so they can move forward in their journey. That's my role. If I can be of any encouragement to anyone, regardless of their backgrounds and/or ethnicity, I will, and I want to be.

My purpose is to help people deal with conflicts in their relationships, either personal or interpersonal, in a marriage or a family, in a healthy way. With deeper understanding of God's love for them and His desire to have a relationship with them, they would be able to deal with and resolve issues and reconcile with themselves, and with each other and ultimately with God. That's my purpose and my future.

T. Cher arriving at the airport in Asia and
preparing to go through customs, 2007

Mai Yia's mother: Iab Vwj Yaj

CHAPTER NINE

My relationship with my wife over the years has taught me a lot about sacrifice, a lot about listening, and a lot about giving. My wife has sacrificed a lot for me. When we got married I was still trying to finish high school. Then I moved on to complete my college education. Instead of pursuing her own career, my wife stayed behind in the home to raise our children and remained beside me to support me, to raise the children, be a mother, a wife, and the anchor in the family so I could devote my time and focus on my education and ministry.

I am grateful to God for her sacrificial giving to me. She has and continues to teach me about listening. This is our thirtieth going on thirty-first year of marriage, and listening is a skill that I feel I am catching up on. Listening is not just a science, but also an art. I have developed an art of listening and I am continuing to develop the art of listening. Listening is not just hearing the words from another person's mouth, but it's actually listening to the meaning of what people are trying to say and the message they are attempting to convey. In essence, listening is paying attention to what the speaker is actually saying, not just hearing his/her voice but also the tone the speaker uses in sending a particular message. If we have good listening skills and know how to use them in our relationships, a lot of interpersonal relationship issues would be minimized. Listening is critical for a marriage relationship to be successful.

My wife has also taught me about giving. She gives of herself to her husband, to her children, to extended family, to friends, and even to strangers. I'm always bragging about her to my colleagues and even strangers. She may be small in stature, but she has a very big heart. I am so grateful for the kind of wife that God has given to me.

MARRIAGE IS NOT A CONTRACT, IT IS A COVENANT...

How do you know whether you have met the right person? This is a very interesting question, and it's a very critical one for that matter. People say that you can tell with a first impression if that person is right for you or not. For me, when I first saw my wife, I liked her, but I didn't realize she was going to become my wife because she initially didn't like me. I believed in my heart, though, that I would be marrying this young woman someday.

But as you get to know a person more, the feeling you have is so much more than just an infatuation. Personality type, character type, attitude type ... these are very important components in a person you need to look for. Then, your guts tell you that that person is the one for you. As Christians, however, as you look for your life partner, you need to make a conscious decision to allow God to be your advisor in choosing your future mate. That would minimize the potential heartache in the days ahead.

And as Christians, we know that marriage is more than a contract, it is a covenant. Because God has a commitment to His people, he covenanted Himself with His people. Go back to the Fall of Adam and Eve and look at the mess they made and how God reacted. Instead of blotting them out of the earth and creating new species, He pronounced the consequences of their disobedience and banished them from the Garden. But before He did that, He showed grace by making clothes for them to cover their shame – "The Lord God made garments of skin for Adam and his wife and clothed them" - Genesis 3:21. Then, as we read further into the future of the human race, God again called a man and made a covenant with him – Noah and his family. After the Flood, God spoke to Noah saying, 'I now establish my covenant with you and with your descendants after you and with every living creature that was with you... - Genesis 9:9-10. Story after story in the Bible depicts God's goodness through His covenant with His people.

A successful and lasting marriage is like that. It is not a contract but a covenant. A contract simply says that two people agree to certain terms and conditions. If any of the terms in the contract are breached by either one of the parties, the violated party has the right to cancel the contract.

Furthermore, a party in the contract has the right to cancel any and/or all terms of the contract with or without cause so as to avoid any major legal complication. So in essence, a contract says, "If you do this for me, then I will do the same for you. We do things equally (50-50).

A covenant, on the other hand, says "I promise to give myself to you and will do for you with all of me to the best of my ability to nurture you, grow you emotionally, psychologically, and spiritually. My goal in doing so is to advance and mature our relationship no matter what." In the Western, Caucasian's wedding vows, those to be married declare that marriage is "for better or for worse, in health or in sickness, until death do us part…" This is what covenant means. Unless, and until, death, you do not part. In a covenantal relationship, both parties remain committed to one another through thick and thin—through the ups and downs of life.

All marriages will have their ups and downs. Sometimes the downs may be more than the ups, but people in covenant will not cut and run when they encounter challenges and difficulties in the journey of their marriages. Instead, they are willing to admit their wrongs and accept responsibility for improving their relationship. [13]

---

13   This portion is taken from my teaching series on Biblical Marriage which I have developed over a period of three years in leading a Monthly Couples Gathering with a small group of friends who desired to cultivate a deeper marriage relationship with their spouses. I am grateful to the Lord God for Numtsheej and Ntsum Xyooj, Vam Suav and Xw Xyooj, Tswv Nplooj and Zuag Xyooj, and others who participated in this series and walked with my wife and me as we explored what Scripture says about Covenant Marriage Relationship.

In a contract relationship, you do 50 percent of the task. In a covenant relationship, one person says, "I will do 100 percent of the task" and the other person will say, "Since you are doing 100 percent, I will also do 100 percent." In a way, both are willing to go the distance.

And so, we need to understand that a marital relationship is not a contractual relationship where you have a marriage license simply signed by a magistrate or a clergy, and if things go well and life is a rose, then you are OK. But when the going gets tough, you quit. That is not what God intended for marriage and society.

My advice is to think carefully and seriously. Make decisions appropriately before you enter into a marriage relationship, because you are entering into a serious relationship that will have life-altering consequences in the days ahead.

When my children began dating, I told them to take into consideration how their relationship or a potential relationship would impact the entire family. I would advise them to introduce their potential date to me in person. I told them, "Remember, your date now may eventually have the potential to impact our relationship as a family because he or she will eventually become part of our family. If she or he doesn't have a proper perspective on me, on your mother, or on your siblings, that would tell a lot about whether he or she would be interested in building this relationship with you or if it was for selfish purposes that this person is trying to court you." This is the same advice I would give to readers, grandchildren, and great-grandchildren.

In my personal experience in the past 30 years as a pastor, finance and communication seem to be the issues that cause the most problems in marriages. But if you look at these issues closely, they are just the symptoms. The real issues are more in the personality type and the misunderstanding of each other's personality types. If we can garner a deep understanding of our spouse, who they are, what makes them tick, and how best to nurture and respond to them, we won't have a problem bringing up issues. If, on the other hand, we don't "go deep" with our spouse in truly understanding their personality type, we will have issues that we don't want to deal with because we may feel threatened that if we bring this issue up, it's going to explode.

And when the issues are not brought up, they only get worse. It can be like a wound that a person has incurred that has become an infection. You know that it hurts and you know that there is something in there causing the infection. Whether it is malignant or whether it is a small object inside, it creates pain. But when you are thinking about taking that object out of that part of your body, the thought of even more excruciating pain crosses your mind, so you decide to just leave it. You let it go and postpone the surgery, if you will. The longer you postpone, however, the more the infection deepens and spreads. And eventually the whole body will be infected by this small, but untreated wound. This is the same situation in the marriage relationship. The longer we wait to talk about issues, the worse they become. So it is important to understand our mate in order to know how best to talk about issues.

Also, I might have some personal issues that are not related to my relationship with my wife, but when she talks to me or acts or thinks in a way that tends to bring out that memory, instead of owning up to my hurt and pain of the past, I tend to point the finger at her and blame her. I may have a feeling that she may be rejecting me and leaving me. Therefore, any time we talk about issues, the closer we come to the issue, the more I back off. I retreat into my own little world to lick my wounds. My advice is that, in any relationship, instead of getting upset with the other, we need to take a look at ourselves and see what is really going on. If an issue stirs up an emotional rollercoaster in me, then I know I must deal with myself before dealing with the relationship issues that I have with my spouse.

T. Cher, Mai Yia and all of the children and grandchildren with Mai Yia's mother, on the front lawn of home in Maplewood, MN, 2011

Chapter Ten

For me, family is a gift from God. As a pastor, a husband, a father, a grandfather, a brother, and a son, the older I get, the more I realize the indispensability of family. My family is what keeps me going. In my life so far, I've raised five adult children and have seven grandchildren. I often told my sons and daughters that I wanted to be the best father I could. But because I grew up as an orphan from a very young age, I didn't have a role model in my life, so I learned to be a father the best I could, as I went.

The older I get, the more I realize that as a father, a lot of times I made wrong decisions. A lot of times I did things wrong. I told my kids that if I had to do it over again as a father, I would do things differently.

I wanted to have the best for my kids, and so I overprotected my children. I was afraid to allow my children to make mistakes. I sheltered them, and I didn't give them room to grow through their mistakes. My children would agree also that their mother and I overprotected them growing up. Those are the regrets that I have still have.

If I had to do it over again, even though a lot of times my emotion would overrule my intellect, I would argue that I would let my intellect take over and let my kids make mistakes. I would not overprotect them. I would not over-shelter them. This is some of the advice I would want to give to my kids, my grandkids, and whoever who may be reading this book.

As I have related earlier, Vaam Pov, my third oldest brother, died in January, 2000. He was a quieter brother, but he was not only a brother, he was also a friend. When we first came to St. Paul, we purchased a duplex together. His family lived upstairs, and we lived downstairs. Pooling the resources we had at the time allowed us to acquire the house we needed to raise our children "under" one roof, while we still maintained our independence as two separate families. We also bought the house together so that Mom could be our childcare provider while all four of us worked to support our families. Unfortunately, he had to move away to Menomonee, Wisconsin.

I will never forget the day he died. I have related the story earlier, but would like to add that his death impacted us as a family and impacted me because it was so sudden. We didn't have any time to grieve, and we were Hmong.

My brother, Nuj Sua, and I were very close. When we each got married and had children, our children were very close. As I related earlier, our families would vacation together. He was a very quiet person, but he and I developed a special relationship. We would call each other almost on a daily basis and ask each other how we were. For any special family trips, we would invite each other and take time out to be with each other and each other's kids.

He was diagnosed with an unknown cancer in October of 2003 and he died in May of 2004. According to doctors, even though his cancer was found on his liver, they didn't know the source. His death really impacted me, more than any other experience that I had had. Maybe I was just getting older and my age affected my outlook on life, but his death, compounded with the death of my brother Vaam Pov a few years earlier, made me a basket case for quite a while. It took a diabetes disease to wake me up from my grieving of my brothers' passing.

My other brother, Num Huas, who is older than I am, is currently living in Menomonee where he moved over two years ago to become a pastor at a Hmong church and also to be closer to family. Num Huas has been separated from the rest of the family for the last 20 plus years, partly because of his ministry assignments, and partly because of personal desire to distance himself from the rest of the family so he could learn about life and independence.

We are grateful to God for granting brother Num Huas a

son in his old age. Pobzeb Isaak was born a year ago. He has been very proud of his new-born son. Num Huas and I used to fight a lot, though, when we were young, probably because the two of us were together more frequently, and we had more time on our hands. As we grew older, we became closer since we went to school together and lived in the same house for four years. We grew to love each other, accept each other, and appreciate each other more, especially now.

My three brothers' deaths actually impacted our family relationship quite significantly. But those of us remaining learned to love each other, and value each other more than we used to in the past.

I want to pay tribute to my parents. My father, I know, loved me very much. I was his baby, and he called me Balau, meaning "Wine" in Lao. My name, Cawv (Anglicized "Cher"), literally means *wine*. So my father, instead of calling me Cawv, called me Balau. It is a nickname that he gave me. He loved me very much.

Without that vivid memory that I had when my father stroked my head back and forth, whispering in my ears that he was going to die, leaving me as an orphan, I wouldn't be the kind of man that I am today, even though he only had one conversation with me and it was a farewell conversation, if you will. That was a defining moment for me as a boy, knowing my father was not going to be with me any longer. That gave me the confidence to be a man, not because I didn't have a father, but because I had a father who had a lot of affection for me and a lot of hope in me.

Mother, Lig Yaaj, St. Paul, MN, 1993

I regret that my father did not live to see the struggles my mother, brothers and I had and the journey we made from those days wandering in Laos, crossing the River and Oceans to the success and prosperity God has blessed us with and the joys we have. My father would have been so proud to see his sons and grandchildren and the success and kind of life and influence that his sons have on others today.

I also want to pay tribute to my mother because she has been the nurturer. She cared for my siblings and me during our formative years, and she served as parent, provider, teacher, disciplinarian, protector, and guide. For that, I'm grateful.

I want to pay tribute to my brothers, also. My two older brothers were the providers, leaders, and protectors for our family. They stood in the gap after my father's passing to take the lead to minimize the potential of us orphaned brothers being threatened in the community. They worked hard alongside my mother to provide food for us in our journeys all throughout our refugee years in Laos and our safe passage to Thailand.

On a spiritual side, I want to pay tribute to my pastor and spiritual father, Dr. Maurice Irvin, and Ken and Nancy Frasier who are still living in Ellison Park, Pennsylvania. They are still very good supporters and encouragers and friends. Maurice has been an inspirational mentor and father figure to me in my ministry journey. In humility, he served the Church very effectively and influenced countless souls for the kingdom of God, including my family and me. For that, I am grateful.

I also want to pay tribute to my wife who is my friend, my life partner, ministry partner, and my soul mate. She has been through thick and thin with me over the years. She continues to put up with me when I become unreasonable and encourages me when I am down. My wife stands beside me as an advisor, counselor, prayer supporter, and a defender. Without her I would not have become the man that I am today.

**Ken and Nancy Fraser, visiting Shell Point
Village in Florida, December 13, 1992**

CHAPTER ELEVEN

There are a lot of people who have shaped my life. From a social perspective, I would say my mother had the most significant influence on me. As I get older, I see my behavior sometimes in my mother and my mother's behavior in me.

My pastor and spiritual father, Maurice Irvin, developed in me a love for God, for the Bible, for reading, and for people. He was the senior pastor of Allegheny Alliance Church in Pittsburgh when we came to the city. He saw potential in me and took a special interest in me, discipled me, and nurtured me. He took me to school and on my behalf, he talked to school administrators, and when I went off to college, he asked the college president himself to take care of me on his behalf.

**Allegheny Alliance Church. T. Cher and Mai Yia were led
to faith in Christ, married, and sent to Bible College.**

Because of that, he has become a second father to me. I remember when we were still in school, and he came to visit us in 1986. I was doing my internship in Milwaukee. We didn't have any money for gas, and before he left, he gave me his credit card and said, "I am going to write a note here for you to take along with this credit card, and whenever you purchase gas or any food on your way and people ask you, you hand them this note saying you have my permission to use the credit card." He has been a source of encouragement, providing for my journey in my education and professional development. I am grateful for his and his wife's generosity.

And then there are Ken and Nancy Frasier who have been good friends and supporters in prayer for us over the last 32 years. They're still praying for us and supporting us in ways we can't even think about, nor can we imagine their love for us. The kindest people in my life, aside from my wife, would be Ken and Nancy. They were members of the Allegheny Alliance Church in Pittsburgh, so we have known them since 1980. When we settled in Pittsburgh, they were some of the first people, besides the pastor, to come into my life. They had been involved with a lot of young refugee people at that time, but they took a special interest in me and eventually my wife. Then they were interested in us not so much as to convert us to Christianity, but they were interested in us as people, and they loved us regardless. Eventually, they became sort of a second set of parents to us.

When we were in Pittsburgh and I was still young and restless and directionless and futureless, I started smoking, because I was influenced by my friends who were refugees like me. One day I remember coming out of my apartment holding a cigarette in my hand. For some reason, Nancy walked by, and she saw a cigarette in my hand. She didn't say much. All she said was, "Cher, did you know that smoking is dangerous to your health?" That comment actually hit me in the head, and I threw that cigarette away. That was the last time I touched any nicotine. That really influenced me to think about my personal health. So Ken and Nancy have been, and continue to be, an important part of my personal and family life to this day.

Keith and Sally Turnbull with Ken and Nancy Fraser, good friends and disciplers from Hmong refugees and their families in the early 1980s at the Fraser's Summer Cottage in Beulah Beach, Ohio

And, of course, my wife has influenced me a lot. She has taught me about being patient and about being able to let go of a lot of things that I thought I wanted, but I didn't have.

My education has also influenced me quite a bit. The opportunities I have had in the classroom and community afford me the ability to think critically and constructively about my past, how I was brought up, and about my present. My personal character also has been shaped through interactions with church leaders and ministry servants, including the Reverend Dr. Billy Graham. It was an honor to share the pulpit with Mr. Graham when the Billy Graham Evangelistic Association conducted a week-long Crusade in the Minneapolis Metrodome in 1996. I had the privilege to pray for the Friday Offering before Mr. Graham preached to over 50,000 people. That was one of the most memorable moments in my ministry life.

Historical figures like Martin Luther King influenced me quite a bit also. The way he led the Civil Rights movement in the 1960s showed me the importance of having values that you are willing to die for. I recall his saying something to the effect that a man who doesn't have anything worth dying for is not worth living. I am still learning what that means. If I don't have any personal conviction that I am willing to give myself to, that tells me a lot about who I am.

Another important person in my life is my mother-in-law. She has been very supportive of me and our ministry through the years. One of the many ways she has endeared herself to me was by giving us our very first car when we were in college. We went into college with nothing, and as we moved to Georgia, she moved from Pittsburgh to East Moline. She knew that we didn't have a car, so she called us and said, "You can come and take the car and use it. You need it more than I do." It was a 1979 Ford Pinto. We used that car for a couple of years when we were in school. My mother-in-law was a part of our lives during our college years, really helping and encouraging. My mother was, as well.

These are the people who are very important, special people in our lives as we've been through professional, spiritual, and personal development over the years.

And I could not talk about my life's influencers without mentioning God. I would have to say that, God (in His three forms...Father, Son and Spirit) and the Bible have been the most influential in my life. And God has used the Bible to be the most influential piece. It was the Bible that changed my life and my outlook. It changed my direction and my passion for life.

T. Cher and Mai Yia with Pa Houa visiting Mai
Yia's family in East Moline, IL, summer 1984

T. Cher graduating from Bethel Theological Seminary, St.
Paul, with Mai Yia, Mother, and Phauj Tshuas Pov Lauj
(who passed away a few years ago in St. Paul), 1994

CHAPTER TWELVE

There are four places that are most important to me that I still remember very vividly. The first one is the village where I grew up, Phou Huard. That was the place where I learned to read and write. That was also the place where my father passed away, so it was a place of loss for me as well as a place for education and gain. I gained self-confidence from that village. I also learned the impact of being orphaned. I learned the impact of becoming a refugee.

The second place that impacted me in my growing-up years was the main military center. Even though it was a military center, it was also an educational center for me. I went to school starting second grade there. That was a place where I ventured out into the world, if you will, and learned to be friends with people whom I had not yet met before, and learned to follow directions from teachers whom I had not known before, and learned to accept my role even though I thought I was the smartest kid in my grade school. I discovered there were people who were smarter than I was, and I learned to accept that.

The third significant place for me was the refugee camp. It served as a place for me to rest and to, in a way, transition from a nomad roaming in the jungle into being in a new, though crammed, environment. The adjustment was significant.

The fourth significant place would be Pittsburgh, Pennsylvania. This is where I had the opportunity to start a new life. I found my significance and purpose there. I came to understand that even though I was stateless, I was not unloved. I may have been a refugee in a foreign land, but I was not the first to be one. I had the opportunity to make life worth living because I was still young and had the physical energy to pursue life. Pittsburgh provided an environment conducive for advancement for me both academically and spiritually.

T. Cher and Mai Yia with Pastor Mike and Vanessa Rice, posing for the new church plant's publicity and prayer cards, St. Paul, MN, May 2004

Chapter Thirteen

Who I am at my core has changed during my life. I used to be a very in-your-face person, and that's a very selfish, even though unconscious, type of behavior. The older I get and the closer I walk with God, I have come to realize the flaws I have in me. I have yielded myself to the teachings of the Bible and the directing of the Spirit of God.

Because of that, my life and my behavior have changed. I have become a more likeable person. I have had people come to me and say they like me when they see my smiling face, that it really encourages them. As I think about that, I wonder what it is in me that would be encouraging for them; I think I would be more of a threat to them!

Through the years, my values have changed drastically. Before I came to know Jesus Christ as my personal savior and Lord, my view of life was limited, my vision was nearsighted, and my focus was narrow. When I became a Christian and a pastor, my values changed from being a Hmong to the Hmong. I became a Christian, a Christ follower, who happens to be a Hmong. Let me explain. It is only natural for a person to have a strong connection with his/her roots. In fact, we need connections to not only survive but succeed in all areas of our lives. However, when those connections become very rigid and extreme, there is no room for relationship outside of one's natural environment, and that can exclude socialization with others.

The purpose of the gospel and the purpose of Jesus coming to Earth was not just to die for the Hmong people or for the Americans or for the Asians or for the Europeans. Jesus died for the whole world. My role is to reach out to everyone who has willing ears to listen and a willing heart to understand.

And so my values have changed from just focusing on a particular people to the whole world. i have also changed from being self-centered to being other-centered. I used to think that I knew a lot. Now I know I don't. I used to think I was wise, that I was smart. Now I know that I may be smart, but I'm not wise, as I still have a lot to learn. I have come to understand the difference between wisdom and knowledge this way: Knowledge is the ability to process information without necessarily the ability to apply the principles of the information needed in a certain context. Wisdom, on the other hand, is the ability to use the processed information for the right condition in the right context.

I used to think that I just needed to teach others and that I didn't need to teach myself. Now I have come to realize that what I teach others has to be lived out in my life. I need to live what I preach. I need to practice what I preach.

So these are my values. My values also now focus on family, on faith, and on friends. If it weren't for my family, I wouldn't be here. If it weren't for Jesus Christ, I wouldn't be here. If it weren't for my friends, I wouldn't be here. I cannot live for me. I live my life for God, for my family, and for others. I do the things I do the way I do because they matter. They matter to my family. To others around me. And most importantly, they matter to God.

Who I am, and what I can do, and what I have accomplished so far, I really am convinced that it is all by God's grace. It is by God's grace and kindness that he superintended my life, that he protected me, and that he delivered me from the jungles of Laos. He took me by the hand across the Mekong River to the refugee camp. He got me into the 747 jet to fly across the Pacific Ocean to America. He delivered me from darkness to light. He gave me meaning and significance. Because of this meaning and significance (that is found in my personal worth which is rooted in the knowledge of God through the Lord Jesus Christ), I have the courage to embark on personal growth, and I have future hope, direction, and purpose in this life and a life to come.

**T. Cher posing with sons Cheng and Joshua at
Cheng's graduation from high school**

When I think of my happiest time, I think of a couple of things. Number one is when I am with my family…my brothers and their families, nephews and nieces and their families, my immediate family – my wife and children and grandchildren. Whether going fishing or going to our cabin up in Milaca, MN, or taking my grandchildren to the Community Center for swimming in town, or going to a family picnic in the summer, these times make me happy. When our children were younger, we made it a conscious decision to take them with us on most trips both near and far. The whole family jumped in the car and traveled to places like California, Colorado, Michigan, Ohio, Georgia, and other places we could afford. Those were our fun times, and our happiest times.

Another happy time for me professionally is when I see people's lives changed. When I see people's relationships restored, and when spouses reconcile their differences and come back together to be moms and dads together to their children, I am happy. Also, when I see donors give willingly and compassionately to help us to meet the needs of the community, knowing that, together we make an impact on the lives of everyday people, whether it big or small, these are some of the happiest times in my life.

T. Cher correcting students' final exams in Asia, March 2007

T. Cher teaching Hmong Church leaders in Asia, 2007

Chapter Fourteen

The darkest moment in my life was when I was in the middle of the Mekong River. That night was the longest night in my life. As my niece and I were floating in the middle of this vast and unforgiving pool of liquid, I had no hope for survival. I didn't know if I would even be alive in the next five minutes.

Then the second darkest period in my life was when my ministry was struggling for survival and my brother was dying from cancer. I felt like the world was caving under me, and I was losing my grip on life. I felt like I was fighting a losing battle. Everything around me seemed to be tumbling down. The end of my world seemed to be imminent, and I felt abandoned by everyone. My wife. My children. My God.

I was so emotionally unstable and depressed. When anyone – my wife, my children, my nephews, my extended family, or my friends – tried to help, I would end up crying. I was an emotional wreck. Whether their comments were positive, affirmative, or critical and negative, I would cry. That may have been a midlife crisis or a combination of crises (with my brother dying of cancer and my ministry falling under me and thinking my future was going to end). Those were the darkest days in my life.

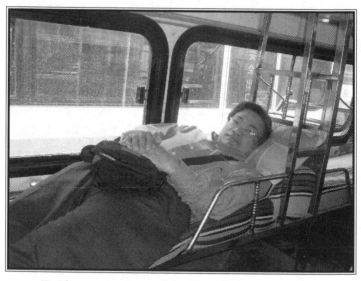

T. Cher preparing to "sleep" in the bus on the way to teaching the Old Testament Survey to Hmong Church leaders at a remote village in Asia, 2007

CHAPTER FIFTEEN

I have learned that difficulty will come. It is not if, but when. When difficulty comes, as Rafiki says to Simba in the movie, *The Lion King*, "You can either run from it or learn from it." I never thought about running away from conflicts, but I didn't know how to learn from conflict, either. But the older I get, the more I realize that when conflict comes, I need to learn from it and adjust myself to, first of all, endure the conflict, and second, to deal with the conflict calmly and intentionally.

When you are emotionally high, meaning when you either are very angry or very excited, your mind is not clear as to be able to make informed decisions. Every decision you make will impact your life in the days ahead whether for good or for ill. One decision that you make can have a potential life-altering impact on you and others around you for the rest of your life and even long after you are gone. You need to make sure that the decisions you make are not based on your emotions, but with your mind, your intellect. That's very important because emotions come and go.

My advice to my children, my grandchildren, or whoever reads this book is that difficult times will pass. As they come, so problems and challenges will also go. There will be challenging times. There will be dark days. There will be turbulent days. There will be tornadoes, thunderstorms, hurricanes, and earthquakes. But those, too, will pass. We all just need to hang tough. And hang tough in the unchanging promise of God that is found in Jesus Christ. The Bible reminds me to "Be still and know that I am God. I will be exalted among the nations. I will be exalted in all the earth" – Ps. 46:10.

Hanging tough, though, without a spiritual anchor, will not last. I have come to understand the Bible verse that Paul the apostle talks about in 1 Corinthians 10:13: "No temptation has overtaken you that is not common to man. God is faithful and he will not let you be tempted beyond your ability. But with the temptation he will also provide the way of escape that you may be able to endure it." The key is to "endure it" and not run away from it before the appointed time – God's appointed time.

So the way to get through difficulties and challenging times is to rely on God. The promise of God is recorded in scripture. Remember, this event, too, will pass, and whatever problems you encounter and no matter how difficult the present crisis may feel or look, eventually you will come out the other end stronger and more polished and skillful and able to face the next challenge of your life again.

T. Cher, Pastor Vam Txos Thoj and other elders baptizing people at Camp JIM (Jesus Is Mine), Brainerd, MN, June 15, 2002

CHAPTER SIXTEEN

Love, forgiveness, anger, reconciliation, and friendship are all very important parts of life. But when left to our own devices, we tend to think that we love others, and a lot of times we do. But unconsciously, we love others because we want something back-- that is the natural inclination. However, Jesus reminded his disciples, and exemplified to them by his death on the cross of Calvary (and to us), that "it is more blessed to give and than to receive" – Acts 20:35.

We are created to love and to be loved. That is the basic human need. All of us as human beings need to be loved. But if we are to be loved, we need also to love without expecting anything back. I know this is easier said than done, but as we progress and as we grow older and are advanced in our years and in our maturity, we will come to understand the meaning of these Scriptural principles and be able to put them into practice.

The Bible says I need to love God with all of my heart and

all of my soul and all of my strength and all of my mind. I need to love God with my total being, and then I need to love others as I love myself. If I don't have a proper love for myself, I would not be able to love others properly or appropriately. Therefore, I need to discover myself in God, through Jesus Christ, as described in the Bible. I need to discover what the Bible says about me and my identity and how God sees me, and then go from there and love myself as God loved me. I would then be able to love others as God would have me love others..

And then there is forgiveness. It is a behavior and an attitude. It is a conscious decision that I have to make whether I want to forgive others or I don't. Forgiving others means that I first have to forgive myself for the many mistakes and wrong decisions and judgments I have made. Baloo the Bear said to himself about himself when Moglee fled from his and Bagira's presence in *The Jungle Book,* "I would never forgive myself if I cannot find Moglee." The challenge for all of us is to forgive ourselves first and then find the grace to forgive others. In order to do that, though, I have to acknowledge God's forgiveness in my life and accept it. Then I will be able to forgive myself and let go of my past and then forgive those who have offended or hurt me and be willing to rebuild the bridge that I may have burned in the process. It has been said that, when we fail to forgive, it is like drinking poison and waiting for the other person to die.

When it comes to anger, you have to understand and recognize that this is an emotion and a part of being human. People in the secular world would say we need to manage our anger. My belief is that the Bible says we can be angry, but we ought not to let the sun go down and still remain angry.[14] Anger can be healthy, but anger can have the potential to be destructive. It is an emotion I, personally, need to recognize. When I get angry, I need to understand why, and I need to know how to control myself in my anger and allow it to teach me how to become a better person.

Reconciliation is very challenging for all of us, especially when we have been wronged. But for your own personal well-being, you need to go and reconcile yourself. First of all, with your inner being, you need to reconcile your feelings, evaluating why you are angry and why you have a conflict inside of you, and making a decision to leave and to let go. Then, make a conscious decision and effort to reach out and reconcile with the other person.

Now the reconciliation process is not just one person's responsibility; it is both parties' responsibility. You may have a desire to be reconciled, but the other person may not want to be reconciled. Therefore, it is a mutual decision to be reconciled by both parties.

While love, forgiveness, and reconciliation are very important, so is faith in God. He has been so gracious, forgiving and willing to accept us for who we are, and He is willing to take us by the hand and transform us into the kind of people he desires us to be. He's faithful, and he is going lead us.

---

14   Ephesians 4:26-27 – Paul the Apostle reminds believers that we can be angry but do not continue to dwell in our attitude of anger long after the sun set, and do not give Satan a single foothold.

CHAPTER SEVENTEEN

In your journey of life, you will encounter others who need love, encouragement, support, and at times, challenge. You need to be a family to those who don't have a family. Support them. Encourage them. Challenge them. Let them know that they are loved by God, the Creator. He desires a personal relationship with them, not just for a time here on earth, but in all eternity. You will make someone's day brighter.

Whatever we do and wherever we go and however far we go, we need to remember that family is very important. Family is the fabric of life.

I once read that if you want to kill your enemy, make him your friend. I am still learning about that. I hope and I pray that my children and my grandchildren and those who would read this will learn to kill their enemy not by bullets or the sword, but their gentle words and charismatic personality to bridge the gap to meet the person's needs.

Make a friend to the potential enemy so that they will then be a friend to you.

I also have come to understand that the individualistic versus the collectivistic ideas are not East versus West so much as a postmodern ideal or philosophical conviction versus traditional values. The industrial revolution that started in the last century and the technological advancements which shrink our world have exacerbated this post-modern lifestyle and value. Hmong people complain to me about the influence and negative impact of the "American relativistic values" on their children, and they bemoan their inability to stop it. My personal observation and experience, however, is that the post-modern, individualistic priorities, rather than the collective priorities, have become the norm, whether here in the United States or elsewhere. And these new priorities are here to stay.

It is important, whether we are Asian or European, or South American, or African, that we promote the family. We have the privilege of being part of a family. With the privilege, though, comes responsibility. We have the privilege of being a son, a daughter, and children of parents. And then we also have the responsibility of being citizens of our country. We are a family member, a community member, and the citizen of a country. And, for that matter, we are a citizen of the world.

We need to take our responsibilities seriously. They are

God-given. And God gives us the blessing of being in this world to enjoy the resources that we have. But we also have been given the responsibility to be stewards of the resources that have been given. Never take God's blessings for granted. And never take your responsibility lightly.

I really believe that in a family, we also are obligated to be stewards of the relationships we have, and we need to put others before us. The Bible says do not just think of and about ourselves, but we should think of others. Philippians 2:3-4 says, "Let each of you look not only to his own interest, but also to the interests of others."

The Bible says we should not do anything from a selfish ambition or conceit, but in humility count others more important than ourselves. Our responsibility is not to just look into ourselves, about ourselves, and around ourselves, but it's to look into others and to see their needs and to meet their needs. As we meet other people's needs, our needs will also be met.

I'm grateful for the opportunity to share my life story. My hope and my prayer is that my life story will inspire, challenge and instruct those who journeyed with me as I crossed the river from darkness to light, from hopelessness to hopefulness, and from purposeless to purposeful living.

T. Cher and Mai Yia, August, 1988, Estes Park, CO.
"Honey, so glad you have chosen to walk this journey with
me thus far. Yes, the journey is still far from over, but the
God's grace and your companionship, we will make it to
our destination – heavenward... until Jesus comes...